PATTERNS OF
FARM FINANCIAL STRUCTURE

A CROSS-SECTION VIEW OF ECONOMIC
AND PHYSICAL DETERMINANTS

NATIONAL BUREAU OF ECONOMIC RESEARCH
FINANCIAL RESEARCH PROGRAM

Studies in Agricultural Finance

1. Mortgage Lending Experience in Agriculture, by Lawrence A. Jones and David Durand

2. Patterns of Farm Financial Structure: A Cross-Section View of Economic and Physical Determinants, by Donald C. Horton

PATTERNS
OF FARM FINANCIAL
STRUCTURE

A Cross-Section View of Economic

and Physical Determinants

BY DONALD C. HORTON

12534

A STUDY BY THE

NATIONAL BUREAU OF ECONOMIC RESEARCH, NEW YORK

PUBLISHED BY

PRINCETON UNIVERSITY PRESS, PRINCETON

1957

Printed in the United States of America
by Princeton University Press, Princeton, New Jersey

NATIONAL BUREAU OF ECONOMIC RESEARCH

FOREWORD

DR. HORTON's study of the financial structure of farm enterprises is one of a series of related investigations made under the National Bureau's Agricultural Finance Project. His principal objectives have been to determine how the economic and physical characteristics of agriculture affect its financing and to describe the roles of credit and equity funds in the financing of agricultural production. Other parts of the Agricultural Finance Project are the following: *Costs and Returns on Farm Mortgage Lending by Life Insurance Companies, 1945-1947*, by R. J. Saulnier (published in 1949); *Mortgage Lending Experience in Agriculture*, by Lawrence A. Jones and David Durand (published in 1954); and *Agricultural Equipment Financing*, by Howard G. Diesslin (published in 1955).

The present study was undertaken and carried forward under a cooperative agreement between the National Bureau of Economic Research and what was then organized as the Bureau of Agricultural Economics of the Department of Agriculture. Through this mutually agreeable arrangement the author had full access to the extensive materials on farm finance available at the Bureau of Agricultural Economics and was able to integrate his work closely with related studies being conducted concurrently at the National Bureau. Resources for the conduct of the National Bureau's part in the study were made available through generous grants of funds from the Association of Reserve City Bankers, the Life Insurance Investment Research Committee acting for the American Life Convention and the Life Insurance Association of America, and the Rockefeller Foundation.

R. J. SAULNIER
Director (on leave), Financial Research Program

NORMAN J. WALL
Agricultural Research Service
United States Department of Agriculture

January 1956

AUTHOR'S ACKNOWLEDGMENTS

IT WAS with the keenest anticipation that I accepted the invitation, offered in 1945, to undertake this study of the system of agricultural finance. The fact that it was to be made jointly by the National Bureau of Economic Research and the Bureau of Agricultural Economics of the Department of Agriculture promised much in the way of facilities for work and opportunity to pursue uninterruptedly a complex problem of primary public interest. From my viewpoint the arrangement has been an eminently satisfactory one, and I wish to express my sincere thanks to both organizations. Particularly, I am grateful to Ralph A. Young and E. C. Johnson, then members of the National Bureau staff, who, with Norman J. Wall—at that time head of the Division of Agricultural Finance of the Bureau of Agricultural Economics, and now head of the Agricultural Finance Section of the Production Economics Research Branch of the Agricultural Research Service of the Department of Agriculture—organized the work in 1945.

As the study has progressed I have been aided by the advice and encouragement of R. J. Saulnier, director of the Financial Research Program of the National Bureau, and F. F. Hill of Cornell University, who has been in charge of the National Bureau's Agricultural Finance Project. In addition to these, many others have contributed generously with ideas, technical advice, and editorial assistance; special acknowledgment is due E. Lloyd Barber of the Bureau of Agricultural Economics and David Durand, Thor Hultgren, and Alvin S. Tostlebe from the National Bureau. The last three named served on the National Bureau's staff reading committee for the manuscript.

My debt to other research workers is a heavy one, though it cannot be indicated by specific reference. A substantial part of the estimates on which the study is based depend on unpublished data and research studies developed over a considerable period of time by my former colleagues in the Bureau of Agricultural Economics and by research workers in the state agricultural experiment stations. I wish, however, to make specific acknowledgment of the use of unpublished county estimates of farm mortgage debt for 1940 prepared by Sarah L. Yarnall, formerly of the Bureau of Agricultural Economics. The identity of much of these materials is lost in the specific estimates used in the study, and, while I am pleased to acknowledge the contribution of Miss Yarnall and of others in the development of this factual basis, I must, of course, accept full responsibility for the estimates and for the analyses based upon them.

Among those who assisted in the assembling and evaluation of data for this study and in the presentation of the materials special acknowledgment is made of the assistance received from Joan Janow Brody and Olive K. Britt of the Bureau of Agricultural Economics, Catherine Martin of the National Bureau, and members of the Bureau's editorial staff.

Donald C. Horton

CONTENTS

CONTENTS

xiv

CONTENTS

TABLES

TABLES

CHARTS AND MAP

PATTERNS OF
FARM FINANCIAL STRUCTURE

A CROSS-SECTION VIEW OF ECONOMIC
AND PHYSICAL DETERMINANTS

INTRODUCTION

BY R. J. SAULNIER

THIS study was undertaken as one of the set of investigations which constitute the National Bureau's Agricultural Finance Project. A recently published study by Lawrence A. Jones and David Durand on *Mortgage Lending Experience in Agriculture* and my own earlier investigation of *Costs and Returns on Farm Mortgage Lending by Life Insurance Companies, 1945-1947* are parts of the same project, as is Howard G. Diesslin's recent monograph on *Agricultural Equipment Financing*. It is perhaps evident without elaboration how these studies and the one in hand can be used in building the Project's capstone volume, now in progress at the National Bureau under the tentative title of "Agricultural Credit Facilities in the United States." Dr. Horton's book is basic to the capstone study: working as close as possible to the level of what the economist calls "real" phenomena, he attempts to show how the physical and economic features of farms are related to the way in which farms are financed. In doing this he contributes much to our general understanding of the agricultural financing process; more specifically, he shows how particular sources of capital and credit are drawn on to meet the needs of particular types of farms, and thereby gives substance to the familiar concept of a "system" of interrelated farm financing facilities.

The author's object does not imply, of course, that the forces shaping agriculture's financial arrangements are to be found exclusively in the physical and economic features of farms. Much less does it imply that there is necessarily any causal connection running from the nonfinancial to the financial features of farms. Yet one can be unduly timid about making inferences of this type, for there is assuredly more reason for believing that financial arrangements accommodate themselves to the nature of the productive process and the conditions under which it is carried forward—no less in agriculture than in industry and trade—than that such connections run in the opposite direction, or that they are absent altogether. As the reader will see, the author speculates on the causal connections between the economic and physical characteristics of farms and farm financial patterns where he feels it is justified, though he is careful not to infer too much from his material. The reader, of course, will not necessarily be subject to equal constraints.

3

The ideal factual basis for a study of this kind would consist of cross-section and time series data on individual farms, but unfortunately such materials are largely unavailable. Bodies of information may be found that give for individual farms many of the characteristics—financial and nonfinancial—pertinent to the present study, but they are fragmentary at best and spotty in their representation of the leading types of farming. The only available data adequate for the author's purposes, and which he was under necessity to employ, are averages for groups of farms, more specifically, averages of the characteristics of all the farms within given counties as of 1939-1940.

The use of county averages in the present analysis obviously involves serious statistical hazards. Perhaps the most important is that the averages for some of the counties may mask appreciable differences in the characteristics of the farms which they encompass, and may not be representative, really, of any significant number of the farms in the county. Another difficulty is that although the essence of the study is to reveal differences in financial patterns systematically associated with economic and physical differences among farms, the portrayal of these differences—which would be a relatively simple matter if one could deal with individual farm units—may be difficult or impossible on a basis of countywide averages. In view of the seriousness of these hazards it may be useful to comment briefly on Dr. Horton's solution of his informational problem.

His procedure was to select, from among 250 counties on which usable information was available, 108 that appeared to be relatively homogeneous internally as regards the physical and economic characteristics of their component farms and that, as a group, gave the widest possible representation of different kinds of agriculture. The test of internal homogeneity was made primarily on the basis of the author's knowledge of the agriculture of different parts of the United States, but certain bodies of descriptive information were available which helped in that connection. While we may be sure that interfarm differences are present beneath the countywide averages, it is believed that neither in kind nor in quantity are they such as to disqualify the data for the analytical purposes to which they are put.

As for the second difficulty, the 108-county sample seems to serve relatively well in representing differences among types of farms. Apart from the internal make-up of the county units, emphasis was placed, as the author puts it, "on diversity of representation rather than on homogeneity." Careful consideration was given to the need for obtaining proper balance within the sample as between different areas of the country and different kinds of agriculture. It cannot be claimed that all varieties of farming are represented, or that the differences among types of farms are in all cases shown in their proper degree. Indeed, the author suggests that the differences among types of farms that are revealed by his data are perhaps an exaggeration of those that exist in reality, but since the purpose of the study is to detect patterns of relationship rather than to weigh any element absolutely, this magnification effect may be regarded as a virtue. Furthermore, there are grounds for believing, as the author specifically demonstrates, that the representation of agriculture as a whole by the sample is remarkably good.

Having selected a sample of counties, the author's next major informational problem was to compile reliable data for each of them on those farm characteristics—financial and nonfinancial—that on a priori grounds seem most significantly related to his problem. Here, also, he was often compelled to improvise solutions to his requirements. Data were assembled from a number of different sources on the essentials: the average amount of physical assets per farm, which serves as a measure of farm size; the composition of farm assets, which is broadly suggestive of the character of farm capital requirements; and the distribution of farm income according to type of product, which is also indicative of the kind of farming involved and accordingly of the type of farm financing problem which is presented. Among the indicators of farm financial patterns are the interests of operators, landlords, and creditors in the physical assets involved, the frequency and extent of use of mortgage credit and of non-real-estate credit, and the relative importance of the various sources—commercial banks, life insurance companies, federal emergency lending agencies, etc.—from which real estate credit and production credit are drawn. As the author indicates, many of these materials are estimated, yet their consistency within the sample of counties, and their prima-facie reasonableness, strongly suggest that they give a faithful reflection of the financial and nonfinancial profiles of a wide variety of farms.

Another informational difficulty confronted by the author, one that is common to all analyses employing balance sheet data in the study of financial problems, should be commented on. Balance sheet data necessarily reflect the net cumulative effect of forces operating on an enterprise from its beginning. In most respects the balance sheet reflects deliberate choice on the part of the farm owner; in other respects, however, it reflects forces which have left their mark on specific balance sheet items quite beyond the farmer's power to interfere. Inflation is an outstanding example of such a force: it expands some elements in a balance sheet while having no effect on others, thereby producing changes in financial proportions that must be clearly separated, at least conceptually, from those that occur as a result of deliberate management decisions. Conversely, deflation and operating losses, even without a general decline in values, tend to reduce certain items and automatically to give greater prominence, as reflected in conventional balance sheet ratios, to others. Thus, equity is eroded by asset deflation, whereas the hard rock of indebtedness may be unaffected. At least in the financial structure of surviving concerns, debt stands out more sharply at the end of a deflationary period than at the beginning. The opposite is observed where balance sheets, as is commonly the case in agriculture, are permitted to reflect inflationary increases in asset values. This effect could be ignored in a cross-section analysis if all farms were equally affected, but not if there is reason to believe that the effect has been felt in different degrees by different farms. The problem is formidable, and inevitable: no year could have been selected which would have avoided it. Accordingly, a technique for correcting this distortion in the data was required. The method devised was to classify the 108 counties into subgroups so that comparisons might be drawn between combinations of counties which are roughly similar in the extent of asset deflation which they experienced in the decade leading up to the year of report, but differ with respect to the specific economic and physical characteristics being studied. For all practical purposes, this procedure made it possible to study the relationships between the financial and nonfinancial aspects of farms free of the distortions produced by differential financial experience.

Only on the information gathered in the decennial Censuses of Agriculture can studies such as Dr. Horton's be built, and when the present one was undertaken, the latest available census was that of 1940. His investigation is based largely, therefore, on data for that year. It would have been interesting to add a similar analysis for 1950, but this was not possible within the resources accessible to the author; however, the census materials are available now and perhaps will at some time be studied by comparable methods.

Even though we lack a comparison as thoroughgoing as the work in hand, the question may still be asked whether the results for 1940 are reasonably descriptive of conditions in 1950 and earlier, and if not, what differences exist. As would be expected, the picture one gets of differences between the farm financial position in 1940 and in earlier and later years is dramatically different depending on whether one looks at the value of farm capital in current or in constant dollars. By the former measure, farm capital was at a very low ebb in 1940, substantially below 1920 and 1950 and almost as low as in 1935. Measured in constant dollars, on the other hand, 1940 is a roughly representative year. These facts are set forth in Alvin Tostlebe's Occasional Paper 44, *The Growth of Physical Capital in Agriculture, 1870-1950* (National Bureau of Economic Research, 1954, p. 40).

But in financial studies there is no escape from dealing with value in "current dollars"; indeed, it is the fluctuations in capital values eliminated by corrections for price changes that comprise much of the substance of financial studies. We must still ask, therefore, whether the relationships revealed in Dr. Horton's study obtained earlier and are likely still to have characterized agriculture in 1950.

Several of the relationships which the author discusses, including the relative use of outside funds and credit, and the sources of credit used, have been examined for 1930 and 1950 and are shown in the following tabulation alongside the 1940 data. Comparison shows, first, that the amount of outside funds employed by agriculture, as a per cent of total assets, was practically

Selected Indicators of Farm Financial Structure,
United States, 1930, 1940, 1950

	1930	1940	1950
Interest in farm real estate of:			
Operators[a]	42.0%	42.8%	53.3%
Landlords[a]	37.9	37.6	39.3
Creditors[a]	20.1	19.6	7.4
Per cent of farms under mortgage[b]	40.1	38.8	27.5
Rates of mortgage debt to value of mortgaged full-owner farms[b]	39.6	42.5	27.6
Per cent of land in tenant-operated farms[b]	31.1	29.4	18.3

[a] Estimates based on data published by the Bureau of the Census and the Department of Agriculture.

[b] Bureau of the Census.

the same in 1930 as in 1940. In 1930, farm operators had a 42 per cent interest in farm real estate, compared with 43 per cent in 1940. Landlords held interests of 38 per cent in both 1930 and 1940, and the interests of creditors in farm real estate were 20 per cent in both years. As would be expected, this relationship was more stable for the country as a whole than for its parts. Moreover, when account is taken of non-real-estate credit—so far as incomplete data permit—creditor interests in total farm assets appear to have declined between 1930 and 1940.

In 1950 the distribution of interests in farm real estate among farm operators, landlords, and creditors was quite different from both 1930 and 1940. Farm operator interests increased to 53 per cent from 42 in 1930 and 43 per cent in 1940; landlord interests rose somewhat to 39 per cent, while creditor interests declined from 20 per cent to 7 per cent. The value of farm real estate rose sharply from 1940 to 1950, reflecting the inflation of this decade, while farm real estate debt declined by $1 billion. The result was that operator equities rose, and creditor interests—both in dollar amount and as a percentage of total assets—were reduced.

A mild counteraction set in during the following years. Between 1950 and 1955, creditor interests in farm real estate increased from 7 to 9 per cent; while the value of farm real estate increased, by 21 per cent, farm real estate debt rose more steeply, by 47 per cent. In the future, as farms change hands on the basis of post-World War II values, the rise of mortgage debt relative to real estate values will tend to continue. Accordingly, the creditor interest in farm real estate was probably lower in 1950, and the interest of operators higher, than will be the case in the future. In other words, there will be a tendency for the situation in future years— barring such events as marked the forties—for the pattern of farm financial relationships to move toward, rather than further away from, the 1940 status.

Second, it is known that both the percentage of farms under mortgage and the ratio of mortgage debt to the value of mortgaged, full-owner farms fell sharply from 1940 to 1950, further reflecting the farm prosperity of that decade. Similarly, the percentage of land in tenant-operated farms fell sharply—from 29.4 per cent in 1940 to 18.3 per cent in 1950—but this decline was offset by a sharp rise in the rented land in farms operated by part-owner operators. As a result, landlord interests in total farm real estate were about the same in 1950 as in 1940.

These comparisons suggest how the pattern of farm financial

organization has been affected by changing economic conditions. Additionally, there is evidence that underlying economic forces are at work tending to alter the financial structure of farms in different kinds of agriculture, quite apart from the impact of depression and wartime inflation. Nevertheless, the evidence strongly suggests—though it is not conclusive on this point— that the relationships characteristic of 1940 have considerable stability over time and provide useful suggestions as to the relationships prevailing around 1950 as well as around 1930.

A further examination of the stability of farm financial relationships was made on the basis of data for individual states. The forty-eight states were arrayed from high to low on the basis of the combined interests of landlords and creditors (outside interests) in farm real estate in 1940. Of the twelve states that ranked highest in this respect in 1940, eleven had been in the top twelve in 1930 and eight remained so in 1950. Of the four states in the 1940 array that did not fall within the top twelve in 1950, three were within the top one half in that year. Similarly, there was a tendency for states that ranked high in 1940 with respect to operator interest in farm real estate to rank high in 1930 and 1950. Maine, West Virginia, and New Hampshire occupied first, second, and third place, respectively, in all three years.

Creditor interests in farm assets in different areas in any given year tend to reflect the immediately preceding economic circumstances. Eight of the twelve states that ranked highest as to creditor interest in 1940 had been among the twelve highest in 1930, but only five of the twelve highest states in 1940 remained among the twelve highest in 1950. As regards the proportion of farms mortgaged, there was considerable duplication of states in the upper one fourth of the array in both 1930 and 1950. None of the twelve highest states in 1940 had ranked lower than eighteenth in 1930, and none ranked lower than nineteenth in 1950.

The differential effects of the depression of the thirties and the inflation of the forties on creditor interests in farm real estate reflect mainly divergent movements of debt and real estate values. This is suggested by a comparative ranking of states in the three decennial years by the ratio of the mortgage debt outstanding to the value of full-owner farms. The states ranking highest in 1940 include several Grain Belt states that were among those that suffered most during the depression of the 1930's. On the other hand, debt-to-value ratios for 1950 reflect the impact of wartime inflation and high farm incomes.

In sharp contrast is the relative stability of state rankings made on the basis of landlord equities in farm real estate. In this respect, Illinois ranked first in 1930 and 1940 and second in 1950. All but two of the twelve states ranking highest in 1940 had been among the twelve highest in 1930, and nine of the twelve remained within the highest twelve in 1950. Landlord equity rankings were far less changeable between dates than debt-to-value ratios. A tendency for landlord equities to bulk large has persisted in certain states, even though they are among the group that suffered most in the 1930's and benefited most from the wartime inflation.

Finally, it may be inquired whether 1940 was an atypical year as regards the distribution of farm mortgage real estate debt among major institutional lender groups. The fact is that the distribution in 1950 was more nearly similar to the distribution in 1930 than to that characteristic of 1940. Between 1940 and 1950, commercial banks, savings banks, and life insurance companies became more important as sources of farm mortgage credit, while federally sponsored agencies became less important. This occurred as the private lenders renewed their farm financing activities after the heavy refinancing operations of the federal land banks and the Federal Farm Mortgage Corporation during the 1930's. Yet the area specialization of life insurance companies changed less over both decades than might have been expected. From 1940 to 1950, life insurance companies came to hold higher percentages of total farm mortgage loans in the Southwest and in other range livestock states, and smaller percentages in the East North Central and southeastern states. But the hard core of life insurance loans in 1950 was still in the midwestern grain states and in the West South Central region.

So much for the central object of the study, the method of analysis, and changes which preceded and followed the base year of the study—1940. What does Dr. Horton's analysis tell us about the influence on agricultural financing arrangements of the economic and physical features of farms? The study reveals many such relationships, primarily between certain patterns of financing and certain combinations of nonfinancial farm characteristics. In other words, there exist both a high intercorrelation of the economic and physical characteristics of farms, such that we can identify a number of fairly distinctive nonfinancial profiles for farms, and certain affinities among sources of capital and credit, such that we can isolate certain fairly distinctive patterns of farm finance.

There are two ways in which the connections between these nonfinancial profiles and financial patterns can be elucidated: one method is to trace the relationship between a particular physical or economic characteristic of farms, or a stated combination of such characteristics, and the financial pattern of the farm; the other is to take a particular financial characteristic, such as heavy reliance on landlord investment, or some combination of such characteristics, and show what types of farms, described in terms of their physical and economic features, are generally financed on this pattern.

Certain fairly consistent relationships are revealed by the first method. For example, the relatively large farms given over primarily to the production of crops and livestock, and on which land is ordinarily a major and buildings a minor component of assets, characteristically make relatively heavy use of external funds, usually drawing on landlords for equity and on such mortgage lenders as life insurance companies for long-term credit. Also, farms of this type ordinarily rely rather heavily on production credit, which they tend to draw from local sources, predominantly from commercial banks and production credit associations.

The rationale of this financial pattern is fairly obvious. The fact that farms are almost invariably owned by individuals means that on those of relatively large size recourse must be had to outside funds. Insofar as equity funds must be obtained from the outside, these must be drawn from landlords, since our financial system provides no other alternative to operator-ownership. To the extent that long-term credit is required, the chances are that this will be drawn from life insurance companies or from the federal land banks, since the farms that conform to the physical and economic specifications set forth in the last paragraph are suited to the investment preferences of these lenders. The investor operating from some distance, whether as owner or creditor, usually prefers, even at some sacrifice of return, to invest fairly large amounts at a time, to make these commitments for relatively long periods, and to rely on the security provided by a lien on land, or more or less indestructible asset, rather than on the potentially transient protection of sound management. In brief, crop and livestock farms of relatively large size both demand external funds and are naturally congenial to their investment on a long-term, absentee basis.

11

Contrasting sharply with the large-scale crop and livestock farms are the large farms in which dairy production predominates. The largest of the farms in this group are still not as large as the largest crop and livestock farms, however, and they make substantially less use of external funds, especially of funds drawn from absentee sources. The equity in them is more likely to be provided by the operator than by a landlord, and there is a somewhat greater tendency to depend on local sources for such long-term credit as is used, rather than on lenders operating from some distance.

These facts, too, are easily rationalized. The fact that dairy farms typically are somewhat smaller than large crop and livestock farms in many cases makes it feasible for the operator to supply the needed ownership funds; and the strategic role of management in the farm's operations, combined with the specialized nature of the assets which it employs, discourages investment by individuals or institutions not in a position to keep the farm's operations under more or less intimate and continuing observation. The fact that dairy farms characteristically make relatively little use of short-term production credit may mean that their working capital needs are minor, in consequence of their more or less regular and constant income, or that their needs for medium-term financing are met mainly by mortgage loans secured by real estate assets.

Finally, fairly consistent financial patterns are displayed by the common types of small farms. One such type is the relatively small farm on which land is a modest component of total assets and on which buildings, consisting predominantly of the farm residence, represent the major form of wealth. It is a further characteristic of such farms that much of the operator's work is done off the farm, and that a high proportion of the farm's product is consumed at home. At most these are part-time farming operations and may, perhaps, be fairly described as being on the borderline between the agricultural and the industrial communities. Farms that fit this description usually make relatively little use of outside funds, except for the financing of the farm residence, a fact which does no violence to their characterization as part-time farming units.

A second fairly conventional type of small farm is that on which dairy, poultry, or miscellaneous products are ordinarily the major source of income. Land is usually a minor, and buildings a major, component of the assets of such farms, but they are more obviously geared to the agricultural process than are the small farms in the first group. On the financial side, they tend to make somewhat greater use of external funds, drawn primarily from local sources and from federal emergency credit agencies. They depend but little on landlord investment and show no noticeable tendency to attract funds from absentee lenders. This pattern of financing clearly reflects the relatively unfavorable income position of these farms, the kinds of assets which they possess, the relatively small amount of funds which they require, and the problems of investment supervision which they present to the potential outside investor.

It must be apparent from what has been said that there is a distinct tendency for the various suppliers of funds for farm enterprises to focus their activities on certain types of farms, in other words, for there to be what Dr. Horton calls a functional specialization of financing facilities. Thus, insurance companies tend to lend where loans of relatively large size can be made, where the security for the loan is an asset relatively indestructible at least in its physical aspect, and, as a corollary of the latter, where it is not necessary to "bank," as the saying goes, on day-to-day management. This combination of asset preferences reflects the nature of the insurance company, and the conditions under which it operates. Being a national agency, in no position carefully to watch the daily operations of management and using funds that can be appropriately invested for long periods, it naturally falls into this functional groove. Its more or less natural companion as a supplier of ownership funds is the landlord, and for reasons that are perhaps obvious.

The commercial banks and production credit associations, on the other hand, are ideally situated, as local institutions, to know and to cope with the problems of farm management, and are predisposed, because of the laws under which they operate and the type of funds which they have to invest, to seek out relatively short-term investments. It is readily understandable, also, that commercial banks and production credit associations, both having relatively severe credit standards, occupy a markedly different functional niche from the federal emergency credit agencies that were set up, and have been administered, to aid farmers in hard-pressed circumstances.

The outstanding fact revealed by Dr. Horton's study concerning federal farm mortgage credit facilities, notably the federal land banks and the Federal Farm Mortgage Corporation, is their apparent lack of functional specialization. In contrast to the private agencies, which seem to have some more or less distinct fields of activity, the federal agencies appear to serve a cross-section of all types of farms. There are a number of reasons for this. First, their facilities are nationwide, and because of their organization they are necessarily under some pressure to lend funds in all areas. Unlike the insurance companies, they are in no position to withdraw from a particular section on the ground that it presents credit risks higher than can be sustained at the rates of interest which they are permitted, or desire, to charge.

Second, the broad participation of the federal land banks in mortgage lending as of 1940 reflects certain historical circumstances. In the early twenties and again in 1929 and 1930 foreclosures eliminated life insurance companies as lenders in certain areas and caused them to concentrate their new lending in relatively limited regions. This created a credit gap which only the subsidized and specially protected federal agencies could fill. Especially in the early thirties, the refinancing on a broad scale by these agencies of farm mortgage loans made originally by private lenders left them with creditor interests in a wide variety of types of farms, many of which credits were still extant in 1940, contributing to the more nearly universal and less specialized nature of the agencies' lending operations.

It is along these lines that the author seeks to show how the pattern of farm financing facilities reflects the nonfinancial characteristics of farm enterprises. The study of agricultural credit institutions will extend the analysis by showing how the organizational characteristics of various farm financing agencies and the types of funds which they employ influence their asset preferences. In this way it is sought to build a fuller understanding of the institutional framework within which the farm financing process takes place, and to win the practical benefits that such an understanding will bring within reach.

CHAPTER 1

PURPOSE AND SCOPE OF THE STUDY

WHEN viewed as individual economic units, farms differ widely in the amount and kinds of assets they use, the nature of their operations and production, the extent to which nonfarm activities are combined with farming, and many other economic characteristics. They also differ widely in the manner of their financing. For example, an owner-operated, debt-free farm presents a pattern of financial organization quite different from that of a farm in which interests are held by the operator, by one or more landlords, and by creditors. Farms also differ significantly in the sources from which they draw their capital, depending on whether these are predominantly local in character—as for example, the farm operator, local landlords, and commercial banks —or are absentee landlords, and institutions such as large insurance companies that are part of a more impersonal, outside capital market. Finally, farms differ in the extent of their relative dependence on short-term and long-term credit, and in the degree to which each of these types of credit is obtained from federal or federally sponsored agencies, from private lending institutions, or from individuals.

The different patterns of financial organization that are found in different sectors of agriculture doubtless reflect a large number of influences, some of which are difficult to identify and evaluate. Many of these influences can probably be identified with the nature of the farm assets and farm operations that require financing. For example, the characteristic size of total assets per farm varies widely among different regions and types of farming. This alone might be expected to influence both the extent to which equity capital can be furnished by farm operators and the interest that absentee investors may have in owning such assets or lending on them. Aside from size of farm enterprise, the kind of assets involved and the nature of the operations probably influence the attractiveness of different types of agriculture for different classes of investors. Farm assets doubtless vary widely with respect to their salability: some may have a fairly broad market and others a rather narrow local market. Extremes in this respect are easily cited: for example, an Iowa cash grain farm in contrast to an Appalachian hill farm. Farms on which success or failure depends heavily on the managerial skill of the operator

15

may require that a relatively large share of the financing be carried by the operator and by local creditors, whereas farms in which success or failure depends more on weather and prices, rather than on day-to-day management, may be better suited to impersonal, absentee equity or debt financing. Such differences in farm assets and operations may go far to explain differences in farm financial organization between general farming and specialized cash grain farming areas. It is with the identification and analysis of influences of this character that this study is concerned.

Certain relationships between the economic nature of agriculture and the financial organization of farms are systematically examined for evidence bearing on the adaptations farm financial organization tends to make to the nature of the agriculture involved. How do size of farm business, nature of assets employed, nature of products produced, and other economic characteristics of the agriculture influence the pattern of farm financial organization? What kinds of agriculture are able to draw both equity and debt capital from a relatively broad capital market? What kinds of agriculture either have little need for, or are unable to attract, investment funds from a broad capital market? What sources of capital are competitive and what sources complementary in different agricultural situations?

Answers to such questions not only will increase our general knowledge of interrelationships between farm financing and the financial system as a whole, but also will contribute to the evaluation of public and private policies in relation to agricultural finance. For example, differences in the nature of agriculture may influence the extent to which equity financing by farm operators is preferable to similar financing by nonoperators. Debt capital requirements may differ among kinds of agriculture to such a degree both in amounts and in the terms and conditions needed that considerable lender specialization may be appropriate in the credit phase of agricultural finance. Some kinds of agriculture may be poorly suited to attract debt capital from institutional credit sources, whereas in other types of agriculture keen competition for loans among a number of institutional lenders may provide abundant credit. Any light that can be thrown on the structure and operations of the agricultural sector of the capital market should contribute indirectly to the solution of a number of specific problems in the field of agricultural finance.

Tracing Relationships between Economic and Financial Characteristics of Agriculture: An Illustration

Before undertaking a description of the data and methods of analysis to be employed, it may be useful to illustrate in broad terms the general character of our analytical problem. This can be done most simply, perhaps, by use of statewide estimates giving, for the year 1940, an approximate percentage distribution of the interests of operators, landlords, and creditors in farm real estate.

These data are given in Table 1, in which states are grouped by broad type-of-farming regions. Because the 1940 distribution of interests in farm real estate doubtless was influenced by financial experience during the 1930's, the percentage reduction in the value of farm real estate from 1930 to 1940 is given for each state. It ranged from less than 10 per cent to more than 60 per cent. In general, severe deflation might be expected to depress operator interests and increase creditor interests, but the effect on landlord interests is less clear. Reduced equities of indebted landlords may have been offset by a larger number of farms becoming landlord-owned as a result of distress transfer of farms of owner-operators to former creditors.

The statewide data reveal certain general relationships between the financial organization of agriculture and the type of farming involved. For example, the eleven northeastern states contrast sharply, in their high operator and low landlord interests in 1940, with the four Great Plains states. A part of the difference in operator interest may reflect the sharp asset deflation in the Great Plains states during the 1930's. Yet Maine and Kansas, which experienced about the same farm asset deflation, reveal sharply contrasting operator and landlord interests in farm real estate. Specific comparisons such as these suggest strongly that regional differences in farm financial organization can be explained in many cases largely by differences in the nature of the assets and production processes characterizing the agriculture in the several regions.

Other comparisons, however, suggest that similarities and differences in the financial organization of agriculture may result from causes other than those assignable to type of farming. For example, relatively high operator interests are found in states that represent rather sharply contrasting types of farming. The sixteen states with highest operator interests in 1940 include not

TABLE 1

Operator, Landlord, and Creditor Interests in Farm Real Estate, 1940, and Deflation in Value of Farm Real Estate Assets, 1930-1940, for States Grouped by Region

	INTEREST IN FARM REAL ESTATE, 1940, OF:			ASSET DEFLATION 1930-1940
	Operator	Landlord	Creditor	
Northeast				
Maine	71.8%	8.2%	20.0%	36.1%
New Hampshire	70.9	11.1	18.0	19.6
Vermont	62.3	12.7	25.0	23.9
Massachusetts	61.8	16.6	21.6	18.8
Rhode Island	61.0	23.4	15.6	23.7
Connecticut	60.7	21.4	17.9	10.0
New York	61.0	18.7	20.3	28.0
New Jersey	56.6	22.0	21.4	23.8
Pennsylvania	61.2	23.6	15.2	28.2
Delaware	52.5	33.0	14.5	18.0
Maryland	52.8	30.5	16.7	23.1
Corn Belt				
Ohio	50.2	33.2	16.6	14.7
Indiana	43.5	37.6	18.9	11.6
Illinois	29.9	53.6	16.5	23.9
Iowa	28.5	45.3	26.2	36.3
Missouri	41.4	37.9	20.7	38.4
Lake States				
Michigan	58.4	22.5	19.1	21.4
Wisconsin	46.2	23.8	30.0	31.4
Minnesota	38.7	35.2	26.1	32.1
Great Plains				
North Dakota	27.5	43.7	28.8	48.5
South Dakota	22.3	52.4	25.2	60.7
Nebraska	25.8	47.0	27.2	54.4
Kansas	31.5	48.5	20.0	37.7
Appalachian				
West Virginia	71.5	20.4	8.1	21.1
Kentucky	58.2	27.7	14.1	10.9
Tennessee	55.3	30.8	13.9	10.6
Virginia	64.6	24.7	10.7	21.1
North Carolina	49.5	38.3	12.2	12.7
Southeast				
South Carolina	46.4%	40.0%	13.6%	10.7%
Georgia	39.7	43.2	17.1	16.8
Florida	56.4	31.9	11.7	23.4
Alabama	40.5	39.5	20.0	18.6
Delta				
Mississippi	37.6	41.3	21.1	16.4
Louisiana	40.0	44.4	15.6	15.4
Arkansas	40.8	43.3	15.9	16.6

(concluded on next page)

TABLE 1 (concluded)

	INTEREST IN FARM REAL ESTATE, 1940, OF:			ASSET DEFLATION 1930-1940
	Operator	*Landlord*	*Creditor*	
Oklahoma-Texas				
Oklahoma	33.4	48.1	18.5	33.1
Texas	38.3	45.0	16.7	28.0
Mountain				
Montana	42.1	39.0	18.9	33.6
Idaho	45.1	31.7	23.2	18.7
Wyoming	42.1	36.5	21.4	23.1
Colorado	36.7	44.0	19.3	38.3
New Mexico	49.3	36.0	14.7	9.8
Arizona	43.9	37.3	18.8	16.6
Utah	55.6	20.7	23.7	30.2
Nevada	51.2	27.3	21.5	25.8
Pacific				
Washington	50.2	31.8	18.0	23.3
Oregon	53.2	27.8	19.0	24.4
California	47.0	34.2	18.8	36.6

Source: Computed from records of the Department of Agriculture, Agricultural Research Administration, and the 1930 and 1940 Censuses of Agriculture.

only nine of the eleven northeastern states but also West Virginia, Virginia, Michigan, Kentucky, Utah, Tennessee, and Florida. And the sixteen states with lowest operator interests include, in addition to the four Great Plains states, twelve others that are rather widely distributed—Iowa, Illinois, and Missouri in the Corn Belt, Minnesota in the Lake states, Georgia and Alabama in the Southeast, all three of the Delta states, Colorado in the Mountain states, and both Oklahoma and Texas. To find reasons for similarities of farm financial organization among these states may require a type of analysis that goes beyond comparisons of type-of-farming regions to similarities in more basic economic characteristics of the agriculture that have a direct bearing on farm capital needs and investor attitudes.

The possible influence of a widely different financial experience in the 1930's on the financial organization of agriculture in 1940 can be illustrated by reference to two Corn Belt states, Ohio and Missouri. It seems probable that the differences between these two states in operator, landlord, and creditor interests in 1940 would have been less if Missouri farms had not experienced much the greater asset deflation. The fact that farm real estate values in Missouri fell by 38 per cent from 1930 to 1940, as compared

19

with 15 per cent in Ohio, suggests that more operator interests were shifted to landlords through distress transfers during the 1930's in Missouri than in Ohio, and also that in Missouri there was a greater increase in creditor interests at the expense of both classes of owners. A similar problem is raised when the distribution of operator, landlord, and creditor interests in 1940 is found to be much the same in Alabama as in Missouri. Alabama's substantially better financial experience in the 1930's may invalidate direct comparison of financial data for these two states. We cannot make valid comparisons of financial organization of agriculture among states in 1940 without taking into account divergences in financial experience during the preceding decade.

Whereas among states in the same general region the proportions of operator and landlord interests in farm real estate in 1940 show a fair degree of similarity, the importance of the creditor interest often varies considerably. For example, creditor interest was much higher in Vermont than in Pennsylvania, in Iowa than in Illinois, in Wisconsin than in Michigan, in Nebraska than in Kansas, in Alabama than in Florida, and in Idaho than in New Mexico. Again, a part of the explanation may be found in divergent financial experience in the 1930's, but it seems improbable that this would be the full explanation.

The foregoing comparisons based on the distribution of interests in farm real estate are perhaps sufficient to illustrate the kinds of analytical problem with which this study is concerned. Although financial data on a statewide basis, such as those presented in Table 1, suggest certain general relationships between type of farming and the financial organization of agriculture, they also indicate that differences in farm financial organization between one area and another reflect specific influences that cannot readily be associated with differences in type of farming. One such influence is the financial experience of an area in the years immediately preceding the date for which data are analyzed. Still others may be discernible by further analysis. If pertinent factors influencing the financial organization of agriculture are not to be bypassed, the study must be developed within a frame of reference broad enough not only to permit recognition of a number of additional interrelated factors but also to permit an analysis of their interrelationships in terms of the operations of the agricultural sector of the capital market.

General Plan of the Study

It is obvious that attainment of the study's objective requires a much more detailed analysis than is possible with statewide data. For lack of adequate information on individual farms, county data have been used.

Within the limits set by the relevancy and availability of information, a sample of 108 counties was selected to insure representation of widely different kinds of agriculture. The data refer mainly to 1940, the only year for which adequate information by counties was available, and have been developed largely from the agricultural census, from materials compiled by lending agencies, and from special surveys. Major differences and similarities in the economic aspects of the agriculture of the sample counties are indicated, and estimates introduced to bring out county differences and similarities in the financial characteristics and capital structure of farming.

The use of county data, which refer, of course, to groups of farms, calls for a word of caution as to the interpretation of the results of the study. Conclusions necessarily refer to sectors of agriculture rather than to individual farms. Averages often are expressed in terms of farms but have meaning mainly as indexes of differences among types of agriculture. Thus, the financial structure of an average farm in almost any county would fit the census definition of a mortgaged part-owner farm—that is, a farm in which interests are held by operators, landlords, and creditors—whereas, in fact, farms with such a financial structure constitute but a small proportion of all farms. Such indexes, however, are believed appropriate for an over-all analysis of how the economic nature of the agriculture of an area influences the pattern of its farm financial structure.

Criteria for analyzing the economic characteristics of agriculture had to be selected for their validity in comparisons of counties with different types of agriculture and in widely separated regions. This imposed rather severe limitations on the kinds of measures to be used, so that of the large amount of information available by counties, much had to be rejected as too specialized. Even more limited are the means for developing financial criteria, but here the principal obstacle is the paucity of financial information.

The agricultural census, lending agency data, and survey estimates referring to county aggregates of farms are examined, in the pages that follow, to determine whether particular patterns of financial organization are consistently associated with particular patterns of farm economic organization. However, no attempt is made to classify counties directly according to predetermined general classifications of farm financial and economic organization designed for the present analysis. Instead, the counties are first classified according to rather specific indicators of the nature of their agriculture and of the financial characteristics of their farms. For an examination of classifications based on these specific criteria, and from general background information on capital sources available to agriculture, an attempt is made to appraise the influence exerted by the economic nature of agriculture on the over-all pattern of farm financial arrangements.

It should be noted, finally, that the attempt to relate these two aspects of agriculture, each so complex in its own right, precludes separate consideration of factors determining the structures of the agricultural economy and of the financial system. For example, it is not feasible to consider here such questions as what determines the amount of assets per farm, why particular kinds of assets are of greater importance in dairy farming than in cash grain farming, and why one type of agriculture is found in one county and a different kind in another. Nor is it feasible to consider the reasons why banks prefer different kinds of earning assets from those preferred by insurance companies. For the most part it is necessary to take such differences as given, in seeking to determine the relationship of the economic nature of agriculture to its financial organization.

CHAPTER 2

DATA AND METHODS OF ANALYSIS

SOURCES and technical details of the data of the study are provided in Appendix A, so that here the description of their character and of the plan of analysis can be aimed at a general understanding of the text. The principal indicators of the asset, product, and financial characteristics of farms that proved useful are discussed in the first two sections of this chapter. In the following section the 108-county sample, on which so much of the study rests, is treated in detail. Next, a description is given of the method used to take account of the fact that during the 1930's the financial experience of the agriculture in some of the counties differed greatly from that in others.

Indicators of the Economic Characteristics of Agriculture

From a fairly long list of available indicators, a few were selected to measure such factors as variations in farm size, in the economic nature of the assets used, in the kinds of farming operations conducted, and in the extent to which the farm and the farm family were involved in nonfarm economic activities. Of course no limited array of measures can reflect all of the many characteristics of agriculture that may be significantly related to the over-all pattern of its financial organization; often, in fact, some of the most significant economic characteristics of a particular sector of agriculture can be imputed to it only by combining a background knowledge of its agriculture with the objective measures chosen. In some connections, the indicators serve more to provide clues to significant differences in the economic nature of agriculture than to measure their precise extent.

FARM SIZE AND ASSET COMPOSITION

Average physical assets per farm has been selected as a measure of farm size. Among total agricultural assets the county estimates include the value of the farm dwelling, but exclude household and consumption goods for lack of adequate data. To make the concept of average farm size conform more closely to the aggregate of resources usually financed in a single business unit, cropper-operated farms in the South are excluded from the total number of farms in that area in the computation of average farm size.

This adjustment is in the direction of defining a farm as an ownership, in contrast to an operation, unit. It is believed that an analysis of the influence of farm size on financing in the Mississippi Delta counties, for example, is more meaningful when the average farm unit is defined in this manner than when it is defined so as to treat the cropper-operated farm as a separate unit.[1]

In any event such estimates of average asset size of farms as can be employed serve more as measures of relative than of absolute size; that they are generally lower than average for commercial farms in the several counties is due to inclusion in that category of many "nominal" farms—part-time farms, retirement farms, and rural residential properties on which some farming is done. In a study of commercial farm financing, it would be essential, of course, to exclude all such units. For the purposes of this study, their presence in the available data is potentially useful in determining whether the over-all farm financial organization of the agriculture of counties in which such agriculture is important differs from that of counties where agriculture is almost entirely commercial. Accordingly, specific measures have been developed to indicate the relative importance of these non-commercial farms in the structure of agriculture.

The estimates that can be made of average farm asset size for 1940 do not permit direct comparison among counties, since relative asset values in that year probably are not representative of long-time relationships among the counties. Real estate values in 1940, and to some extent other farm asset values, were still affected by the differing impact of the depression of the 1930's in different localities. Hence intercounty comparisons of farm asset size must be confined to individual counties that had a roughly comparable financial experience, or to county groups with a roughly similar mix in that respect. The techniques applied are discussed later in the chapter.

Five indicators are employed to provide uniform breakdowns of agricultural assets in the sample counties. Two of them—the percentage of total physical assets in land (excluding buildings) and the percentage of total acreage in cropland—provide partial bases for comparisons of the importance of land, and of the kinds

---

[1] Even as adjusted, the census data may understate the average asset size for some of the southern cash-crop counties in comparison with cash-crop counties in the North. It is true that eliminating the cropper-operated farms entirely in computing the averages is an overcorrection for this one factor, but the inclusion of all tenant-operated farms probably more than compensates for it.

24

of land, in the asset structure of farms. Another—the percentage of total physical assets in buildings—also provides, in conjunction with other indicators, an indirect clue to type of farming. The percentage of total real estate value in farm dwellings is useful as a measure of the relative importance of "nonfarm" assets. Finally, the percentage of total physical assets represented by items other than real estate—livestock, equipment, and other working capital—provides a general indicator of the relative magnitude of farm working capital assets.

FARM PRODUCT CHARACTERISTICS

Since the type of operation in which the farm is engaged, as well as the extent and nature of the assets utilized, can reasonably be expected to influence farm financing, indexes are given which reflect differences in the types of products produced on the farms of the sample counties. Census figures on the gross value of products sold, traded, or consumed by the farm household in 1939, distributed by major categories, are presented to indicate the character of the "gross product throw-off." Gross value of product per farm could be used also as a measure of farm size, but less satisfactorily in some respects than average asset size, since it does not reflect differences in nonmonetary income, such as housing services, and may vary widely among counties owing to weather and product-price conditions.

Value of product represented by sales of crops will usually not be shown separately, because agriculture devoted mostly to crops fed on the farm to livestock for sale as meat animals is indistinguishable therein from range livestock agriculture. Instead, sales of crops are combined with sales of livestock exclusive of livestock products, and given as a percentage of total value of product. The percentage of total acreage in cropland is used to distinguish agriculture in which growing of crops is dominant from other kinds of agriculture. Dairy product sales are shown separately, and the remainder is broken between all other product sales (including sales of poultry and poultry products) and farm products consumed by the farm family. The value of farm housing services cannot be shown directly, but its comparative weight is indicated indirectly by the importance of residential property in total farm real estate in 1930. Likewise, though the value of farm family income from off-farm work cannot be measured directly, its relative importance in the various counties is indicated by the average number of days of off-farm work per farm operator.

DATA AND METHODS

To illustrate how the several economic indicators, considered as a group, reflect major differences in type of agriculture, estimates for five counties are shown in Table 2.[2] Physical assets

TABLE 2

Economic Characteristics of Agriculture, Five Selected Counties

(*dollar figures in thousands*)

| | TYPE OF AGRICULTURE | | | | |
| | Large-Scale[a] | | | Small-Scale[b] | |
	Wheat	Range Live-stock	Dairy	Dairy	General
Physical assets per farm	$39.1	$38.5	$17.2	$3.7	$3.9
Physical assets in:					
Land	74%	46%	30%	31%	53%
Buildings	8	8	47	31	24
Non-real-estate	18	46	22	38	23
Cropland/total acreage[c]	72	2	55	27	39
Dwellings/farm real estate, 1930	6	7	28	22	20
Farm product value, 1939:					
Crops and livestock	93	94	44	20	63
Dairy products	1	1	39	47	6
Poultry and prod. and misc.	3	....	10	4	11
Used by farm household	3	5	7	29	20
Off-farm work in days, 1939[d]	16	33	49	52	62
Change in phys. asset value, 1930-1940	–8%	–29%	–16%	–44%	–25%

[a] Large-scale counties are: wheat—Adams, Washington; range livestock —Elko, Nevada; and dairy—Chester, Pennsylvania.
[b] Small-scale counties are: dairy—Ashland, Wisconsin; and general—Pike, Indiana.
[c] Cropland excludes plowable pasture.
[d] Per farm operator.
Note: Data in this and all subsequent tables are for 1940 unless otherwise indicated.

per farm varied in these counties in 1940 from almost $40,000 to less than $4,000, and correspondingly wide variations will be noted in the composition of assets and the pattern of product throw-off. These and other indicators provide concrete bases for the grouping of counties according to common characteristics of their agriculture.

[2] The percentage decrease from 1930 to 1940 in the aggregate value of land, buildings, livestock, and implements and machinery is used as an index of the immediately previous financial experience of the different counties and groups of counties.

Indicators of the Financial Characteristics
of Agriculture

A general indication of county variations in the financial organization of agriculture, and indirectly of the kind of market from which capital is supplied to different types of agriculture, is provided by a distribution of the interests in farm physical assets in 1940 of operators, landlords, and creditors. For example, high operator interests may reflect a tendency for asset ownership and active management to be performed by the same individual, whereas high landlord interests are likely to reflect a greater separation of ownership from management. High creditor interests reflect the provision of capital by nonoperators on a nonownership basis under conditions of greater protection to the investor. Means of measuring this three-way distribution of interests in total physical assets were developed in the belief that in over-all comparisons among counties they would reveal significant adaptations of the financial organization of agriculture to the economic nature of the assets and operations involved.

Even for such general use, this three-way distribution of interests in assets has many limitations. For example, it does not disclose variations among counties in the underlying rental and credit arrangements; unfortunately, data are not available for studying the financial structure of agriculture according to the tenure of the farm operator. Furthermore, the economic functions performed by operators, landlords, and creditors are not the same in all counties. Finally, the analysis is not adapted to showing a typical distribution among these three interests for individual farms in the several counties. Accordingly, the three-way distribution of interests gains in significance when considered along with other indicators of variations in farm financial characteristics.

Financial indicators for county groups of farms are, of necessity, approximations based on data of varying quality. The interest of operators is defined to include equities in both real estate and non-real-estate assets, whether they are a part of the operator's own farm or not, but it excludes his creditor interests in other farms.[3] Creditor interests are defined to include all debts that can be regarded as claims against farm operators and farm businesses. Landlord interests are made up mainly of equities in farm

---

[3] No comprehensive data are available on the creditor interests of farmers in other farms, but they are not believed to be large.

real estate but also include the residual equity in non-real-estate assets after independent estimates have been made for operator and creditor interests.

To provide further financial indicators, census data on farm mortgage debt for owner-operated farms by county have been supplemented with special sample survey data to produce estimates of the percentage of all farms under mortgage, and of the ratios of mortgage debt to the value of mortgaged farms and of all farms. In addition, the distribution of farm mortgage debt among different lender groups has been estimated from various sources and an approximation made of the relationship of the non-real-estate loans of four major institutional lender groups to farm non-real-estate assets.

The fact that these specific indicators of differences in farm financial organization are most meaningful when employed as a group, and when used to differentiate between broad patterns of financial organization, is illustrated in Table 3, where they are applied to five counties selected for widely disparate financial patterns. The first county is one of those in which operator interests in physical assets were highest in 1940. Despite heavy asset deflation in the 1930's the creditor interest is no higher in this than in the second county, chosen from those in which landlord interest in physical assets was highest. Local lenders, such as banks and individuals, held a higher proportion of the farm mortgage debt in the first than in the second county, and the fact that a relatively high percentage of the mortgage debt in the first county was held by the federal land bank and the Federal Farm Mortgage Corporation probably reflects its worse-than-average financial experience in the 1930's. The general picture presented by the first county, therefore, is of a kind of agriculture drawing equity capital to finance real estate from rather restricted local sources, principally the farm operator's own funds, and debt capital from local lenders and governmental credit agencies. The second county appears to draw more of its capital from a broader, more impersonal, and more exclusively private capital market.

The third county resembles the second in the importance of operator as against landlord equities, but has a much higher creditor interest, 43 per cent as compared with 18 per cent. This high creditor interest is at least partly a result of the very sharp reduction in asset values in the 1930's, brought on by several

TABLE 3

Financial Characteristics of Agriculture, Five Selected Counties

	COUNTY CHARACTERIZED BY:				
	High Operator Interests in Physical Assets (Ashland, Wis.)	High Landlord Interests in Physical Assets (Douglas, Ill.)	High Creditor Interests in Physical Assets (Logan, Kan.)	High % of Real Estate Loans Held by Banks (Kent, Del.)	High % of Real Estate Loans Held by Insurance Companies (Coahoma, Miss.)
Interest in physical assets of:					
Operators	76%	31%	23%	51%	23%
Landlords	6	51	34	32	47
Creditors	18	18	43	16	30
Mtgd. farms/all farms	45	45	52	39	65
Mtg. debt/value of mtgd. farms	49	38	59	41	37
Mtg. debt/value of all farms	19	17	24	17	28
Farm mtg. debt held by:					
FLB's and FFMC	58	41	79	18	21
Ins. and mtg. investment companies	5	47	....	....	50
Commercial and savings banks	16	....	4	47	4
Individuals and miscellaneous	21	12	17	35	25
Non-real-estate loans, as % of total non-real estate farm assets, of:					
Banks and PCA's	2	15	31	6	25
FSA and ECFL Division of FCA	3	1	31	3	1
Change in phys. asset value, 1930-1940	-44%	-11%	-57%	-27%	-9%

years of drought, which also helps to explain the extensive use of credit from federally sponsored agencies.

The fourth and fifth counties make an interesting contrast. As of 1940, about half of the farm mortgage debt in the fourth county was held by banks, whereas about half of that in the fifth county was held by insurance and mortgage investment companies. Farm financial organization in the county in which banks were prominent real estate lenders resembles, more closely than in others, that of the county with high operator interests, though the one is in Delaware and the other in northern Wisconsin. And the fifth county has a number of financial characteristics in common with the second—both appearing to draw heavily on outside capital, i.e. on capital in addition to that of farm operators—although one is in East Central Illinois and the other in the Mississippi Delta.

The principal deficiencies of the data available for the description of farm financial organization relate to the use of cross-sectional data in exploring the sources of farm capital, a problem of interpretation inherent in any attempt to study capital sources by means of balance sheet data. Clearly, the fact that landlords had a high percentage interest in the agricultural assets of a county as of a particular date does not tell what percentage of investment there over any definite period of time was made by landlords. On the other hand, it is presumptive evidence of a tendency for farms to be financed extensively by nonoperating owners, as is confirmed by an analysis which showed that there is a correlation between the averages, for the 108 counties of the sample, of the percentage of farms operated by tenants in the six census years 1920, 1925, 1930, 1935, 1940, and 1945 (an indirect indication of the importance of landlord investment) and their ratios of landlord interests for 1940.

The most serious distortion in the 1940 cross-sectional data has already been referred to, namely the influence of differential financial experience during the depression years of the 1930's. The assumption made in this study is that even though underlying patterns of financial structure in agriculture are modified by changing economic conditions, important continuing differences among counties are likely to be found if allowance can be made for the shorter-run influences stemming from general economic conditions. It is assumed further that the major short-run influence to be considered in the use of data for 1940 is the wide divergence among counties in financial experience in the 1930's, and a method has been devised to take account of its effect.

Characteristics of the 108-County Sample as a Whole

The 108 sample counties, whose location is shown in Chart 1, were selected from a list of 250 for which survey data on mortgage credit and related financial information were obtained on a sample basis for 1940 with the object of representing as many different kinds of agricultural situations as possible.

First consideration in selecting counties had to be given to the quality of the available data, and a large number of the 250 were eliminated on this basis alone. Other were eliminated because they were so mixed as to type of farm that averages would have little meaning, or in order to retain a better balance by areas and kinds of agriculture. In the final selection an attempt was made to include counties within broad type-of-farming regions representing diverse subtypes of agriculture, as well as counties representing the major type of farming of the region, and thus to emphasize diversity of representation rather than homogeneity.

This method of selection may actually overemphasize the element of dissimilarity: thus, when measured by the several indicators described earlier, differences between the highest and the lowest 36 counties of the 108-county sample tend to be in sharper contrast than those that would be observed between the highest and lowest one third of all agricultural counties in the United States. But to the extent that this happens, the basis for selection facilitates the analysis by accentuating those differences in farm economic and financial characteristics on which the investigation focuses.

While the sample was not intended to typify the entire agriculture of the United States, the comparisons shown in Table 4 indicate that it is not altogether ill fitted for this purpose. In fact, a fair measure of agreement is found when the indicators for the combined 108 counties are compared with corresponding indicators for the United States.[4] Since the sample data have not been used to develop national estimates, the main significance of this agreement lies in the assurance that extreme counties are fairly well balanced in the sample.[5]

[4] If a closer approximation of the sample to the United States figures had been considered desirable, it could have been accomplished by including more general farming counties in the North and omitting some of the larger-scale cotton counties of the South.

[5] It does not follow that equally good results would be obtained for a

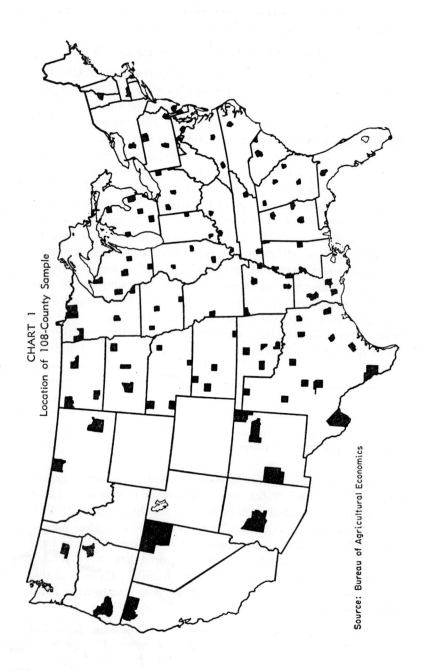

CHART 1
Location of 108-County Sample

Source: Bureau of Agricultural Economics

TABLE 4

Averages for 108-County Sample and for the United States

(*dollar figures in thousands*)

	108-County Sample[a]	United States[b]
Economic Characteristics		
Physical assets per farm	$8.3	$8.0
Physical assets in:		
Land	52%	52%
Buildings	23	24
Non-real-estate	25	24
Cropland/total acreage[c]	40	38
Dwellings/farm real estate, 1930	16	15
Farm product value, 1939:		
Livestock	25	23
Crops	38	40
Dairy products	13	14
Poultry and prod. and misc.	6	9
Used by farm household	18	14
Financial Characteristics		
Interest in physical assets of:		
Operators	48%	} 77%[d]
Landlords	29	
Creditors	23	23
Farms with operator interest in real estate/all farms	63	67
Farms with landlord interest in real estate/all farms	50	44
Mtgd. farms/all farms	43	40
Mtg. debt/value of mtgd. farms	40	42
Mtg. debt/value of all farms	19	20
Farm mtg. debt held by:		
FLB's and FFMC	47	41
Ins. and mtg. investment companies	12	15
Commercial and savings banks	10	8
Individuals and miscellaneous	31	36
Non-real-estate loans, as % of total non-real-estate farm assets, of:		
Banks and PCA's	13	13
FSA and ECFL Division of FCA	8	5

[a] Counties are given equal weight in the averages except in physical assets per farm, where the average is weighted by the number of farms. In all averages involving number of farms, the number excludes cropper farms in the South.

[b] Compiled from the Census of Agriculture and records of the Department of Agriculture.

[c] Cropland excludes plowable pasture.

[d] Comparable breakdowns of owner equities are not available for the United States.

33

Although an attempt was made to select counties from most of the major type-of-farming regions, it was not possible to develop a sample that would permit valid comparisons among and within different farming regions. At an early stage of the study it was hoped that the available data would permit such comparisons, but preliminary analyses on this basis encountered a number of difficulties. The counties for which data were available often were not representative of an entire farming region. Furthermore, variations in financial and economic characteristics of the agriculture among counties within a region often were as great as variations among county groups when classified by region. Likewise, counties in widely different farming regions were often found to be much alike as regards certain basic financial and economic characteristics of their agriculture. These results raised considerable doubt as to the significance of comparisons among farming regions for this study, even if the data had sufficed. For these reasons the characteristics of agriculture and of its financial structure that can be compared without direct reference to farming regions have been made the primary basis of the classification of counties for analytical purposes. Very few of the comparisons based on regional and intraregional classifications of counties are presented.

It would have been desirable, however, to supplement the analysis with detailed comparisons of counties within farming regions, and attempts at such an analysis were made, even with the inadequate data that were available. Although the results were often suggestive of possible refinements in the conclusions reached, they have not been presented because of their voluminous nature and of what, in many cases, is a dubious statistical validity. Their main significance lies in the finding that the discernible relationships within regions resembled those that are revealed when regional groupings are ignored and comparisons are made within the entire 108-county sample. The intraregional phase of the analysis is an area that must await development of better basic data.

Adjustment of Sample Data for County Differences in Financial Experience, 1930-1940

Differences in previous financial experience complicate the problem of determining at a given point in time whether there is

---

regional comparison, since no attempt was made to provide a balanced sample for each region.

any tendency for counties with similar patterns of agriculture to have similar patterns of farm financial organization. For example, one would not expect a North Dakota wheat county affected by severe drought and low wheat prices during the 1930's to exhibit a farm financial organization in 1940 similar to that of an Oklahoma wheat county that largely escaped those difficulties. In the first county, operator interests would have been largely lost through forced sales and the shrinkage of asset values; on the other hand, creditor interests, as well as landlord interests in foreclosed farms, would be relatively high. An index of the degree of financial distress experienced in the 1930's is needed, therefore, to classify the counties observed as of 1940 into groups representing different degrees of farm financial distress.

If annual data on farm income had been available by counties, it would have been possible to compare county income levels in the 1930's with those of some previous period; alternatively, financial statistics on distress farm transfers, or debt defaults, might have been used. No usable county data of these types are available, however, and the index of variation in financial experience which was adopted—partly because of the availability of comparable data for the two dates—is the percentage change from 1930 to 1940 in the value of farm real estate, livestock, and equipment. This is referred to as the index of farm asset deflation.

An assumption implicit in the choice is that changes in farm asset values from 1930 to 1940 resulting from increases or decreases in physical inventory would not seriously distort the index for its intended purpose. It is possible, however, that the 1930 and 1940 figures do, to some degree, reflect changes in physical inventory and for this reason tend to exaggerate intercounty differences in financial experience. For example, some of the Great Plains counties doubtless had less land in use in 1940 than in 1930, and their inventories of livestock and equipment may not have been rebuilt by that time. At the other extreme, in some counties land values fell very little and real investment in agriculture rose even during the 1930's, partly as a result of a more favorable economic climate. In effect, however, since the index is not used to make detailed comparisons among individual counties, but rather to classify counties into a few groups according to their financial experience, its deficiency is mainly that it provides a less sharp demarcation than might be desired at the borderlines of major groups of counties.

For almost any date that might be selected, the financial experience of different counties during the preceding ten years would be expected to vary widely. The following distribution of the 108 counties by percentage change in value of physical assets of farms between 1930 and 1940 gives an idea of the extent of variation for the period in question. It should be noted that dif-

PERCENTAGE CHANGE IN VALUE OF PHYSICAL ASSETS, 1930-1940	COUNTIES	
	Number	*Per Cent*
45.0% and more decrease	13	12%
30.0 - 44.9	20	19
15.0 - 29.9	35	32
5.0 - 14.9	24	22
Less than 5.0 decrease and increase	16	15
	108	100%

ferent indicators of the economic and financial characteristics of agriculture may vary widely in the extent to which they are distorted by variations among counties in previous financial experience. Indicators based on numbers of farms, for example, are less influenced by this factor than those based on values. Thus, one would expect to find less distortion of the percentages of farms under mortgage than of the ratios of mortgage debt to the value of mortgaged farms. Evidence corroborating this assumption is furnished by Chart 2, in which the counties are distributed by mortgage frequency, and next by the mortgage debt-to-value ratio, with the 1940 figure to be read on the vertical axis and the average for 1920 and 1930 on the other.

Further corroborative evidence that these two financial indicators are likely to be affected differently by extremes of financial experience in the 1930's lies in certain comparisons of the counties when they are classified according to change in value of farm physical assets during the 1930's. The percentage of the counties in which mortgage debt frequency for owner-operated farms was higher in 1940 than the average for 1920 and 1930 is shown on page 38 by three "asset-deflation" groups of counties.

In the middle group of 59 counties, in terms of extent of asset deflation in the 1930's, higher debt frequency ratios are found in 1940 than in the earlier period in 68 per cent of the counties as compared with 57 and 58 per cent of the two extreme groups. But this difference is not particularly striking, in view of the widely different financial experience of the county groups in the

CHART 2

Percentage of Owner-Operated Farms Mortgaged, and Ratio of Mortgage
Debt to Value of Mortgaged Full-Owner Farms, 1940, Compared
with Average for 1920 and 1930 in 108 Sample Counties

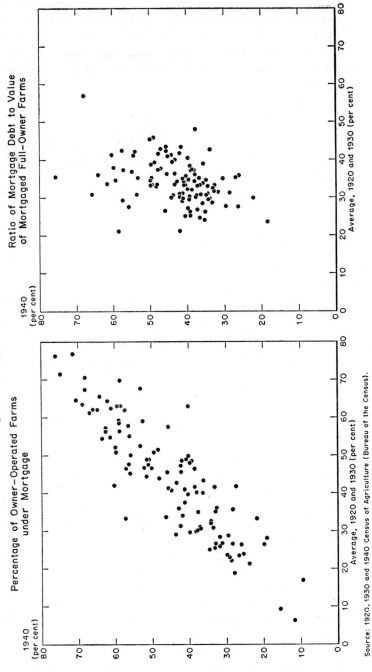

Percentage of Owner-Operated Farms
under Mortgage

Ratio of Mortgage Debt to Value
of Mortgaged Full-Owner Farms

Source: 1920, 1930 and 1940 Census of Agriculture (Bureau of the Census).

1930's. These data suggest that direct 1940 comparisons of mortgage debt frequency among groups of counties differing substantially in their previous financial experience could be made with a fair degree of confidence that financial experience in the 1930's is not the major factor affecting the relative levels of debt frequency in 1940.

PERCENTAGE CHANGE IN VALUE OF PHYSICAL ASSETS, 1930-1940	NUMBER OF COUNTIES	PER CENT OF COUNTIES WITH HIGHER MTG. DEBT FREQUENCY IN 1940 THAN FOR AVG. 1920 AND 1930	DEBT-TO-VALUE RATIO	
			Avg. 1920-1930	*1940*
30.0% and more decrease	33	58%	33%	50%
5.0-29.9	59	68	35	41
Less than 5.0 decrease and increase	16	57	34	35
	108	62%		

But similar confidence is not warranted in direct 1940 comparisons of counties as to the ratio of mortgage debt to the value of mortgaged full-owner farms. To illustrate this point, average debt-to-value ratios for 1940 and for 1920 and 1930 combined are given above for the counties grouped into asset-deflation classes. It is apparent that the ratio of debt to value in 1940 tends to vary directly with the extent of asset deflation in the 1930's.

When 1940 comparisons were made between pairs of counties differing widely with respect to their previous financial experience but little in terms of the nature of their agriculture, it became evident that differences in certain aspects of farm financial organization are fairly consistently related to differences in the severity of financial conditions in the 1930's. Since the presentation of these numerous paired comparisons would be cumbersome, and would invite bias in the selection of counties to be compared, a simple summary form of tabulation had to be devised. The method used was to select groups of counties for comparison that are roughly comparable—as groups—with respect to the farm asset deflation which they experienced in the 1930's.

In the early stages of the analysis, the 108 counties were classified into four equal groups of 27 counties each, based on the percentage change in the value of their farm assets from 1930 to 1940, and these asset-deflation quartiles were then studied separately. An example of this analysis is given in the tabulation below, in which the counties are classified first by degree of asset deflation and then according to average farm asset size—high, middle, and low. Within each asset-deflation quartile, the nine counties with highest average farm asset size are compared with the nine having the middle and the lowest average farm asset size.

FARM ASSET DE-FLATION GROUP (PER CENT)	CLASSIFICATION BY ASSET SIZE OF FARM WITHIN ASSET-DEFLATION GROUPS			
	Largest	*Middle*	*Smallest*	TOTAL
Under 10.0 and increase	9	9	9	27
10.0-22.2	9	9	9	27
22.3-34.1	9	9	9	27
34.2 and over	9	9	9	27
Total counties	36	36	36	108

The county grouping in asset-deflation quartiles was well suited to the conduct of exploratory analyses, but in presentation would involve an unwarranted amount of detail. A summarizing method was found which revealed most of the relationships between the economic characteristics of agriculture and its financial organization shown by the quartile procedure and at the same time greatly simplified the presentation. With the counties arranged as above—each asset-deflation quartile divided into "high," "middle," and "low" groups of nine each according to some economic or financial characteristic—the final step is to combine the four "high" groups, the four "middle," and the four "low." The effect is to produce three groups of counties, of 36 each, similarly stratified as regards farm asset deflation. In a sense the procedure may be described as an adaptation of partial correlation to the special needs of this study, in that it tends to keep average asset deflation relatively constant while other factors vary.

This method of handling the asset-deflation factor is illustrated in the two tables that follow. The object of the first is to discover any relationship that may exist between the extent of operator interest in physical assets and two economic characteristics of the farm enterprise—the percentage of physical assets in land and the percentage of acreage in cropland; of the second, to discover any relationship that may exist between the ratio of real estate debt to the value of all farm real estate and two economic characteristics—the percentage of physical assets in land and the percentage of total product obtained from crops and livestock.

In the first table an inverse relationship is evident in each asset-deflation quartile between the degree of operator interest in physical assets and both the land component of physical assets and the acreage component of cropland; but the second table reveals no consistent pattern of relationship between the ratio of real estate debt to the value of farm real estate and the farm economic characteristics examined. The significant point for present purposes is that these two results—the inverse relationship of the first, and the lack of consistent relationship in the second, are consistent with what is found when the counties are combined, as in the "total" group at the bottom of each table, so as to eliminate the effect of differential prior financial experience.

FARM ASSET DEFLATION GROUP AND INDICATOR	CLASSIFICATION OF COUNTIES BY OPERATOR INTEREST IN PHYSICAL ASSETS			
	High	*Middle*	*Low*	*Average*
Under 10 Per cent and Increase				
Per cent of operator interest	67	49	32	49
Per cent of physical assets in land	47	57	63	55
Per cent of acreage in cropland[a]	34	40	37	37
10.0-22.2				
Per cent of operator interest	66	54	38	53
Per cent of physical assets in land	33	47	64	48
Per cent of acreage in cropland[a]	44	44	51	46
22.3-34.1				
Per cent of operator interest	64	51	42	52
Per cent of physical assets in land	44	49	57	50
Per cent of acreage in cropland[a]	32	34	40	35
34.2 and Over				
Per cent of operator interest	56	36	29	40
Per cent of physical assets in land	47	59	59	55
Per cent of acreage in cropland[a]	33	39	57	43
Total, All Counties				
Per cent of operator interest	63	47	35	48
Per cent of physical assets in land	43	53	61	52
Per cent of acreage in cropland[a]	36	39	46	40

[a] Acreage in cropland excludes plowable pasture.

Partial correlation might have been used if a more precise description of relationships had been necessary, and if the data had been adequate. This would have avoided certain minor defects of the method actually used which may result from giving equal weight to each of the four asset-deflation quartiles when the range of asset deflation is wider in the two extreme quartiles than in the two middle ones. For the possible undesirable effect of giving equal weight to each of the four quartiles, the ratio of real estate debt to the value of mortgaged farms provides the best illustration. Tabulations not reproduced here show that when counties are classified according to debt-to-value ratios in 1940, they tend also to be grouped according to asset deflation

FARM ASSET DEFLATION GROUP AND INDICATOR	CLASSIFICATION OF COUNTIES BY REAL ESTATE DEBT AS A PERCENTAGE OF VALUE OF ALL FARM REAL ESTATE			
	High	Middle	Low	Average
Under 10 Per cent and Increase				
Mtg. debt/value of all farms	20	15	11	15
Per cent of physical assets in land	56	55	55	55
Per cent of product from crops and livestock, 1939	76	63	60	66
10.0-22.2				
Mtg. debt/value of all farms	21	17	13	17
Per cent of physical assets in land	50	43	51	48
Per cent of product from crops and livestock, 1939	62	56	56	58
22.3-34.1				
Mtg. debt/value of all farms	26	17	14	19
Per cent of physical assets in land	43	51	57	50
Per cent of product from crops and livestock, 1939	56	58	68	61
34.2 and Over				
Mtg. debt/value of all farms	28	23	17	23
Per cent of physical assets in land	56	56	54	55
Per cent of product from crops and livestock, 1939	71	66	65	67
Total, All Counties				
Mtg. debt/value of all farms	24	18	14	19
Per cent of physical assets in land	51	51	55	52
Per cent of product from crops and livestock, 1939	66	60	63	63

in the 1930's, with the result that the "high" and "low" counties—
on the basis of a debt-to-value ratio—in the first and fourth
quartiles are likely to differ more with respect to asset deflation
than the "high" and "low" counties in the two "middle" quartiles.
Perhaps the weight given the first and fourth quartiles in the
36-county averages should be less than that given the two middle
quartiles, but this refinement would be of minor importance in
the present study, particularly in view of the imprecise nature of
much of the basic data. Alternatively, the weighting bias pre-
sumably might have been avoided in good part if the counties
had been grouped into asset-deflation brackets of equal range;
but this would have introduced certain mechanical hindrances
to classifying each asset-deflation group according to the various
economic and financial criteria. The decision to use equal numbers of counties as the basis for subclassification was based
primarily on the need for a simple device that would permit easy
and numerous manipulations of the basic data.

It should be noted, further, that the effectiveness of the stratification technique varies with the degree of correlation between
asset deflation in the 1930's and the particular criterion used to
classify the counties. This point may be illustrated by two exam-
ples. The ratio of mortgage debt to the value of mortgaged farms
in 1940, we have seen, is directly related to asset deflation in the
1930's. Thus when the 108 counties, unstratified as to asset
deflation, are grouped into high, middle, and low counties according to their average debt-to-value ratios, the asset deflation indexes
vary correspondingly.

	High	Middle	Low
Ratio of debt to value of mortgaged farms	50%	39%	31%
Farm asset deflation, 1930-1940	37	20	9

If the stratification technique were completely effective, each
of the three groups of counties arrived at by this method should
show an average asset deflation of 22 per cent. The actual results
are as follows:

	High	Middle	Low
Ratio of debt to value of mortgaged farms	48%	40%	32%
Farm asset deflation, 1930-1940	26	21	19

The difference between the high and the low group with respect
to asset deflation is greatly reduced by the stratification procedure,

without greatly altering the difference between the high and the low group with respect to the ratio of debt to value of mortgaged farms; but the high and the low group are still not entirely comparable with respect to asset deflation. Even so, comparisons can be made among the three groups with respect to debt-value ratios on the assumption that the differences shown are not greatly influenced by differential financial experience in the 1930's.[6] For readers who may want to know to what extent the results obtained when counties are grouped without regard for asset deflation are altered by the stratification method used in this study, information is given in a footnote to each major table.

As can be seen from the foregoing discussion, the object of the method selected is not to place individual counties on a comparable basis in 1940; rather, it is to obtain groups of counties that are reasonably comparable with respect to their average prior financial experience. Because the index of differential financial experience employed is the change in the value of physical assets, the method is most effective in making allowances for the effect of extreme declines in the value of physical assets on estimates of farm asset size and on ratios based on asset values. It also enables the analyst to take account of the frequent close relation between the use of federal and federally sponsored lending facilities and the extent of the financial distress experienced by different counties in the 1930's. The effects where other indica-

[6] The failure of the stratification method to produce three groups of counties with precisely the same average asset deflation in the 1930's results in part from restricting the number of initial asset-deflation subgroups to four consisting of 27 counties each. When the 108 counties are classified according to asset deflation into 36 groups of 3 counties each, and then each 3-county group is divided into the high, middle, and low county, the three 36-county groups obtained when all high, middle, and low counties, respectively, are combined, compare closely as regards average asset deflation in the 1930's with the average for the unstratified array. The results of such a tabulation are shown below:

	High	Middle	Low
Ratio of debt to value of mortgaged farms	46%	40%	34%
Farm asset deflation, 1930-1940	21	23	22

It will be noted, also, that the spread between debt-value ratios for the high and the low groups is reduced from 19 points in the case of the unstratified array to 12 points in the above tabulation. Although the difference between the two tabulations *reflects* the correlation between debt-to-value ratios and asset deflation in the 1930's, it does not purport to *measure* the extent to which the ratios in the unstratified array are influenced by differential asset deflation. Other possible influences are not neutral in the two tabulations.

tors are involved are not always so clear, partly because extremes of financial experience may set in motion counteracting influences with respect to particular financial indicators. Thus, landlords with mortgage debts who retained their farms in a period of financial distress would show reduced equities as a result of declining values, but many owner-operated farms were foreclosed and became landlord-owned, in many cases largely free of debt. At the opposite extreme, if economic conditions are favorable many farms may be bought by owner operators, thus reducing the landlord interest in total farm assets at a time when other landlords, continuing their ownership, may be increasing their interest by repaying debt. Since the net effect of differential financial experience on some of the indicators used in the study cannot be separately evaluated, it was believed preferable to allow for these influences by making comparisons among groups of counties that had approximately equal financial experience during the 1930's. In this way, whatever influence the financial experience of the depression decade had on the several indicators would be similar in each of the stratified thirds of the sample.

One further aspect of the method should be made explicit. The method may be described as the use of a dual basis of classification which holds average asset deflation in the 1930's relatively constant by groups of counties. It follows that in the stratified array the 36 counties that are "high" according to a particular criterion (e.g. the percentage of farms under mortgage) may include some that would not be in the "high" group in an unstratified array. The three stratified groups, however, include counties that are predominantly "high," "middle," and "low" in an unstratified array, and when considered as groups, without reference to the individual counties of which they are composed, show distinct differences with respect to the particular criterion which they are intended to reflect. As the averages shown for stratified groups are not used to measure the absolute amount of variation among counties in respect to particular financial or economic characteristics, any distortion of the single classification arrays by the use of dual bases of classification does not impair the usefulness of the data for their intended purpose.

To avoid any possible distortion of results arising from this feature of the summarizing technique, the four 27-county groups (quartiles) representing different levels of asset deflation in the 1930's were first studied independently. These detailed analyses often suggested alternative tabulations that promised results better suited to the analysis. Although these more detailed tabulations could not be presented in each case, a comparative examination of selected farm economic and financial characteristics by asset-deflation quartiles is included for some of the analyses.

Because of the nature of the available data, comparisons of individual counties and groups of counties were first made under tentative hypotheses regarding possible relationships between specific economic characteristics of agriculture, taken separately, and specific aspects of its financial organization. It was soon evident, however, that no single characteristic of a business as complex as farming could provide an adequate explanation of variations in financial organization. Rather, it was necessary to look for significant clusters of economic characteristics that, viewed collectively, are related to significant clusters of financial characteristics of farms.[7] The material presented in the following chapters represents a selection and grouping of such of these comparisons as lend themselves to meaningful economic interpretation.

[7] For many kinds of analysis a geographical grouping of counties based on the concept of "type of farming" has been found to produce significant clusters of economic characteristics of agriculture. This concept, however, does not result in classifications of counties that can be compared advantageously with respect to the financial characteristics of agriculture.

CHAPTER 3

THE RELATIONSHIP OF THE ASSET CHARACTERISTICS OF AGRICULTURE TO FARM FINANCIAL ORGANIZATION

IN ORDER to demonstrate the relationships between the asset characteristics of agriculture and the patterns of farm financial organization that are pertinent to the present analysis, comparisons among counties can be developed from such data as (1) the average asset size of farms in the counties (2) the proportions of farm assets which consist of land, buildings, and non-real-estate assets; (3) the proportion of acreage in cropland; (4) the proportion of assets represented by cropland value; and (5) the proportion of farm real estate represented by the farm residence. Differences among counties in respect to these criteria often reflect other associated differences among farms viewed as economic units, and the relationship between a particular asset characteristic of farms and farm financial arrangements must be interpreted with an awareness that a combination of several related factors, some of which may not be susceptible to precise measurement, may actually exert the controlling influence. For this reason, evidence of a tendency for a particular farm asset characteristic to be associated with a particular financial characteristic is usually not as sound a basis for conclusions regarding causal connections as evidence of reasonably consistent relationships between patterns of interrelated economic characteristics and patterns of interrelated farm financial characteristics.

Relation of Asset Size to Financial Organization

Where differences are found among counties in the average asset size of farms, differences will ordinarily appear in other aspects of their agriculture. Even so, there is some reason to believe that the financial organization of farming may be systematically related to the asset size of farms. Capital requirements per farm would be expected to influence the extent to which farm operators are able to supply their own capital, and size of farm alone may have a bearing on the attractiveness of different sectors of agriculture for landlord investment or for mortgage investment by an absentee credit agency. But since it is not feasible to hold other farm economic characteristics constant while relating asset size to farm financial characteristics, the tabulations presented will include information on certain of those other factors. Comparisons will be more detailed here than elsewhere in the study, in order to acquaint the reader at the outset with the nature of the data used throughout. Data are presented in three ways: (1) using four pairs of sharply contrasting counties; (2) comparing, from an array of the 108 counties by degree of asset deflation in the 1930's, the nine counties of each quartile having the highest assets per farm with all counties in the quartile; and (3) combining the nine counties that are highest in asset size within each quartile, and similarly the nine middle and the nine lowest, thus comparing three 36-county groups similarly stratified as to previous financial experience.[1]

FOUR PAIRS OF CONTRASTING COUNTIES

The pairs of counties in Table 5 are drawn from areas different in characteristic type of farming. They were selected for wide variations in average asset size between the members of a pair, but without wide differences in financial experience in the 1930's except in the case of Pair III, where the worse experience of the one county should be kept in mind.

Even a casual inspection of Table 5 indicates that the counties making up the four pairs differ in more respects than in the asset size of their farms. In the counties with large farms, land tends to be high and buildings low in per cent of total physical assets. Except in the fourth set, which includes a predominantly range livestock county, a higher proportion of cropland to total acreage is associated with higher average assets per farm;[2] and, similarly, the larger-farm counties derived a relatively high proportion of their farm income from combined sales of crops and livestock. These observations will suffice, perhaps, to show that when comparisons of the financial organization of agriculture are made among counties contrasting in average asset size of farm, it cannot be assumed that their agriculture differs economically only in that one factor.

[1] The presentation is designed also to bring out some of the problems that arise in making allowance for differential asset-deflation experience in the 1930's. For (2) and (3) the research methods are those described in Chapter 2.

[2] Percentage of acreage in cropland has different meanings in describing the assets of range livestock and of general farming counties. For this reason several indicators of the nature of farm assets are needed to differentiate among kinds of agriculture.

TABLE 5

ECONOMIC AND FINANCIAL CHARACTERISTICS:

Four Pairs of Counties Selected for Contrasting Farm Asset Size

(*dollar figures in thousands*)

	PAIR I		PAIR II		PAIR III		PAIR IV	
	Douglas, Ill.	Trumbull, Ohio	Coahoma, Miss.	Warren, Miss.	Adams, Wash.	Douglas, Ore.	Webb, Tex.	Upshur, Tex.
Economic Characteristics								
Physical assets per farm	$28.5	$5.7	$24.4	$3.0	$39.1	$7.8	$37.9	$2.8
Physical assets in:								
Land	71%	34%	69%	53%	74%	61%	75%	55%
Buildings	13	42	17	22	8	20	4	24
Non-real-estate	16	24	14	25	18	19	21	21
Cropland/total acreage[a]	82	41	71	17	72	12	3	31
Dwellings/farm real estate, 1930	7	29	16	23	6	12	3	26
Farm product value, 1939:								
Crops	70	23	88	47	86	20	35	41
Livestock	17	10	1	9	7	28	59	8
Dairy products	4	37	1	5	1	10	4	10
Poultry and prod. and misc.	3	11	b	2	3	26	b	3
Used by farm household	6	19	10	37	3	16	2	38
Off-farm work in days, 1939c	21	86	11	37	16	60	48	37
Change in phys. asset value, 1930-1940	—11%	—13%	—9%	—4%	—8%	—28%	—3%	—7%

(concluded on next page)

48

TABLE 5 (concluded)

	PAIR I		PAIR II		PAIR III		PAIR IV	
	Douglas, Ill.	Trumbull, Ohio	Coahoma, Miss.	Warren, Miss.	Adams, Wash.	Douglas, Ore.	Webb, Tex.	Upshur, Tex.
Financial Characteristics								
Interest in physical assets of:								
Operators	31%	72%	23%	54%	46%	70%	41%	60%
Landlords	50	11	46	24	39	14	46	22
Creditors	19	17	30	22	15	16	13	18
Mtgd. farms/all farms	45	42	65	26	47	45	27	21
Mtg. debt/value of mtgd. farms	38	42	37	35	28	34	14	30
Mtg. debt/value of all farms	17	17	28	15	14	17	11	9
Farm mtg. debt held by:								
FLB's and FFMC	41	29	21	40	57	41	27	67
Ins. and mtg. investment companies	47	d	50	d	21	6	d	d
Commercial and savings banks	d	12	4	53	d	6	d	11
Individuals and miscellaneous	12	59	25	7	22	47	73	22
Non-real-estate loans, as % of total non-real-estate farm assets, of:								
Banks and PCA's	15	7	25	21	9	9	8	10
FSA and ECFL Division of FCA	1	1	1	6	4	1	0	20

a Cropland excludes plowable pasture.
b Less than 0.5 per cent.
c Per farm operator.
d No loans reported in the sample.

Evidence that differences in asset size and in farm financial structure may be related can be sought, first, in the relative importance of operator, landlord, and creditor interests in farm physical assets. In all cases, low operator and high landlord interests in physical assets are associated with high average asset size of farm. One would expect large farms to depend more heavily than small farms on nonoperator capital, in view of the ordinarily limited resources of individual farm operators; but it is interesting to note that this means mainly a greater dependence on landlord capital. The data for these selected counties reveal no consistent tendency for counties with large farms to exhibit a greater reliance on credit than those with farms of smaller average size.

A second consistent relationship revealed by Table 5 is apparent in the frequency with which mortgage debt is encountered on the farms of the several counties. In each of the four pairs of counties, the percentage of farms under mortgage is higher in the county with larger farms, though with differences among pairs in degree of contrast. This latter fact suggests that frequency of mortgage debt may be affected by other characteristics of agriculture as well as farm size.

A third relationship can be observed, in the connection between farm size and the ratio of mortgage debt to the value of mortgaged farms. In three of the four pairs of counties in Table 5, the ratio of mortgage debt to value is lower in the large- than in the small-farm county, and in the one case in which the relationship is the reverse the difference is not marked. It should be noted also that in Pair III the higher ratio shown for the small-farm county includes the influence of that county's relatively greater asset deflation in the 1930's. Large farms would be expected to show a higher frequency of mortgage debt than small farms as a consequence of more of the owners' having to resort to borrowed capital; but it is not at once apparent why large-farm counties should have relatively lower debt-to-value ratios. The explanation of differences in debt-to-value ratios may lie in differences, not alone of asset size of farms, but of associated asset composition and product characteristics.[3] This point will be considered again at a later stage in the analysis.

[3] A part of the explanation may be found also in the differing extent to which real estate is used as security for general purpose loans. Operators who own their farms may use real estate as security for loans to finance operating capital; and a relatively large percentage of small farms are owner-operated. On the larger farms, where operators are less likely to own the

There seems to be no entirely consistent pattern revealed by the four pairs of large- and small-farm counties as regards the relative importance of various sources of mortgage credit. In the two pairs of southern counties, federal land bank and Federal Farm Mortgage Corporation loans were a larger proportion of the total in the small-farm counties, whereas in the two northern pairs the reverse was true. But except for the Texas counties, where no insurance company or mortgage investment company loans were reported in the sample data, insurance companies seem to have been relatively heavy lenders in the large-farm counties and banks in the small-farm counties.

Finally, there appears to be no consistency of relationship between farm size and the degree of dependence on different types of non-real-estate lenders.

This limited evidence concerning the relation of farm size to farm financial organization can be summarized by stating that in contrast to the agriculture of small-farm counties that of the large-farm counties tends (1) to be financed to a lesser extent by operator investment, (2) to be characterized by relatively high frequency of farm mortgage debt, and (3) to depend more heavily on insurance companies for real estate credit. Stated another way, the capital structure of large-unit agriculture is characterized by relatively high nonoperator interests (landlord and creditor), and the private mortgage credit used appears to be drawn more largely from absentee institutional investors who operate in a relatively broad capital market. Small-unit agriculture, on the other hand, appears to be financed to a greater extent by operator's equity, supplemented by mortgage credit from local lenders, notably commercial banks. While this general pattern emerging from the evidence provided by four selected pairs of counties is of interest, firm conclusions cannot be based entirely on such limited evidence.[4]

COMPARISONS WITHIN ASSET-DEFLATION CLASSES

The question of the relation between asset size of farm and farm financial organization can be approached in another way,

---

real estate, they may tend to use non-real-estate assets more frequently as security for such loans.

[4] The limitations of comparisons based on pairs of counties are apparent, yet in the exploratory phases of the study they yielded tentative hypotheses which suggested other lines of study. They also provide an element of concreteness that is lacking when groups of counties are compared. To avoid undue repetition, however, comparisons based on paired counties will be confined to only a few selected cases.

namely by grouping the 108-county sample into four asset-deflation classes, as described in Chapter 2. The 27 counties in each quartile were arrayed by farm asset size and the economic and financial characteristics of the agriculture of the 9 counties in each quartile having the largest assets per farm were compared, on the basis of selected indicators, with the average for the entire 27 counties, taken as 100. Table 6 thus permits a determination of the extent to which the financial characteristics of the large-farm counties in each asset-deflation quartile differ from those of the quartile group as a whole.

It is at once apparent that in each asset-deflation quartile the nine counties that had the largest assets per farm were somewhat above average in the importance of land in physical assets, of cropland in total acreage, and of sales of crops and livestock in total value of product. Except for those in the first quartile (greatest asset deflation), the counties high as to asset size were below average in operator equity in assets.[5] As to landlord equity, however, they were higher than the average in all four quartiles. The foregoing relationships parallel those observed for the pairs of counties compared in Table 5.

As in previous comparisons, creditor interest in the agriculture of large-farm counties does not appear to differ consistently from that in other counties, but frequency of mortgage debt is consistently higher than the average. Again, as in the case of paired counties, there is no clear evidence of a consistent relationship between asset size of farm and ratio of mortgage debt to the value of mortgaged real estate. In the first and fourth quartiles this ratio for the nine counties with larger-than-average farms was definitely lower than average, but in the second quartile it was higher (108), and in the third quarter it was only slightly below average (98). Taken together, the four groups high as to asset size had a slightly below average debt-value ratio (97).

With respect to sources of credit, the divergences of the large-farm county groups from the respective quartile averages conform in general to what was found for pairs of counties in Table 6.

---

[5] In the first quartile there was less difference in asset size between the high group and the quartile as a whole than was true for other quartiles. Its high group also experienced less asset deflation in the 1930's than the average for the quartile—41 as compared with 46 per cent. It is possible also that the economic disorganization associated with sharp deflation of assets and income in the first quartile tends to overshadow longer-run influences on the distribution of equities between operators and others.

TABLE 6

ECONOMIC AND FINANCIAL CHARACTERISTICS IN RELATION TO:

Farm Asset Size, Nine Counties with Highest Assets per Farm Compared with Quartile Groups of Counties Ranked by Asset Deflation

| | NINE COUNTIES WITH HIGHEST ASSETS PER FARM (AVG. FOR RESPECTIVE QUARTILE GROUP = 100) | | | | |
| | Asset-Deflation Quartiles[a] | | | | AVERAGE OF QUARTILES |
	1st	2nd	3rd	4th	
Physical assets per farm	169	200	179	228	194
Physical assets in land	108	102	117	115	110
Cropland/total acreage[b]	110	112	126	108	114
Farm product value, 1939, in crops and livestock	115	121	116	126	119
Interest in physical assets of:					
Operators	101	86	91	83	90
Landlords	105	122	111	131	117
Creditors	93	107	109	95	101
Mtgd. farms/all farms	110	111	116	113	112
Mtg. debt/value of mtgd. farms	91	108	98	90	97
Farm mtg. debt held by:					
FLB's and FFMC	98	94	105	88	96
Ins. and mtg. investment companies	143	133	182	158	154
Commercial and savings banks	94	70	74	65	76
Individuals and miscellaneous	85	107	75	103	92
Non-real-estate loans, as % of total non-real-estate farm assets, of:					
Banks and PCA's	110	85	126	113	108
FSA and ECFL Division of FCA	47	79	58	23	52

[a] The 108 counties were arrayed by degree of asset deflation in the 1930's, from greatest to least, and divided into quartiles.

[b] Cropland excludes plowable pasture.

That is, the large-farm counties used insurance company mortgage funds to a greater extent, and bank mortgage funds to a lesser extent, than average. Again, no clear-cut pattern emerges for the federal and federally sponsored mortgage agencies or for the residual group that includes individuals. But except in one quartile the large-farm counties appear to have obtained more-than-average amounts of non-real-estate credit from banks and production credit associations, and in all four classes they used substantially less-than-average amounts from emergency credit sources. Evidence from the paired-county comparisons is conflicting with respect to the latter relationships.

The quartile classifications in Table 6 also illustrate the kinds of data that have been combined into major groups for purposes of comparison elsewhere in this study.[6] In most instances it has been possible, using asset-deflation classes, to combine the nine high counties of each quartile into a new 36-county group consisting predominantly of counties high in the specified characteristic, without dimming those relationships that are clear-cut in the separate treatment. Where the evidence based on separate quartile analysis is inconclusive, it usually remains so in the 36-county comparisons. Comparisons of the latter type are presented next.

THREE GROUPS OF COUNTIES

An advantage of arranging the 108 counties in three groups of 36 each is that errors in basic estimates may be mutually compensating within groups of counties. Even more than the separate quartile analysis, however, the procedure obscures the separate influence of regional differences on farm financial organization.[7] Its main feature is that in retaining the quartile basis of selection, the effect of previous financial experience on the matters at issue is as nearly eliminated as possible, so that the average change in value of physical assets from 1930 to 1940 is approximately equal for each of the three groups of counties.[8]

Before examining the relation between farm asset size and the financial characteristics of the agriculture by means of 36-county groups, it will be necessary to examine how the method of removing the effect of previous financial experience may have affected the results obtained. Accordingly, average values for selected economic characteristics are shown in Table 7 for the "high," "middle," and "low" thirds of the sample as selected (1) by asset size alone, and (2) by asset size within quartile divisions according to degree of asset deflation in the 1930's.

[6] The averages for the combined 9-county groups in Table 6 provide one basis for a summary comparison of the 36 counties that are high as to asset size of farms with the entire 108-county sample. An alternative basis for this comparison is given in Table 8.

[7] The use of 36-county groups raises the question whether regional differences, as such, are controlling in farm financial organization. If this were so, one would not expect to find consistent relationships between farm economic characteristics and farm financial organization in a nonregional analysis of this type. On the other hand, consistency of relationships in such an analysis does not necessarily rule out regional influences since these may be implicit in classifications by nonregional characteristics.

[8] See Chapter 2 for a discussion of this procedure.

Average asset deflation for the entire sample and for the 36 counties with largest average assets per farm (regardless of previous financial experience) was about 22 per cent; but for the middle third it was 29 per cent and for the low third, 15 per cent (Table 7). Stratifying the counties first into asset-deflation quartiles, then arraying them by asset size of farms, and finally forming a "high" group out of the nine high counties from each quartile, and likewise a "middle" and "low" group, brings average asset deflation for all three of the new 36-county groups into substantial equality. In the process, however, average asset size per farm is reduced slightly in the middle group and raised slightly in the low group. In general, of course, the effect of the stratification is to reduce the difference between the highest and lowest groups of counties in respect of the variable being arrayed, in this instance, asset size of farm. But here the effect is slight, and is also minor with regard to economic characteristics of the agriculture. In this case, therefore, stratification produces three groups of 36 counties each that continue to differ sharply in regard to average asset size of farm, without significantly distorting the other economic characteristics of the agriculture.

Examination of the data on 36-county groups in Table 8 suggests, in broad outline, economic and financial relationships similar to those brought out by comparisons of paired counties and those between nine-county groups and quartile averages. On the economic side, large-farm counties are characterized by (1) a high proportion of assets in land, (2) a high proportion of acreage in cropland, (3) a low ratio of value of farm residence to total real estate value, (4) high crop and livestock sales in relation to total product value, and (5) a relatively low home consumption of farm products. On the financial side, large-farm counties, in comparison with the other groups, are characterized by (1) heavy dependence on landlord investment and comparatively low operator interest, (2) high frequency of use of mortgage credit, (3) heavy use of insurance company mortgage funds, (4) less use of bank mortgage credit and (5) light dependence on non-real estate loans of the emergency type.

On a number of the points with respect to which the data for individual counties and for quartile groupings showed mixed results, the 36-county group data reveal little difference, on the average, between large- and small-scale farming (Table 8). The ratio of mortgage debt to the value of mortgaged farms, for example, was 39 per cent for both the large- and the small-farm

TABLE 7

ECONOMIC CHARACTERISTICS IN RELATION TO:

Farm Asset Size, 108 Counties, Regrouped to Equalize Asset Deflation, 1930-1940

(dollar figures in thousands)

	HIGH 36 COUNTIES		MIDDLE 36 COUNTIES		LOW 36 COUNTIES	
	Before Regrouping	After Regrouping	Before Regrouping	After Regrouping	Before Regrouping	After Regrouping
Change in phys. asset value, 1930-1940	-22%	-21%	-29%	-23%	-15%	-22%
Physical assets per farm	$15.5	$15.5	$7.5	$7.3	$3.8	$4.1
Physical assets in:						
Land	58%	57%	50%	50%	49%	49%
Buildings	18	19	25	26	25	25
Non-real-estate	24	24	25	25	26	26
Cropland/total acreage[a]	46	46	42	42	33	33
Farm product value, 1939:						
Crops and livestock	75	75	61	60	53	54
Dairy products	12	12	15	15	13	13
Miscellaneous	4	4	9	8	5	6
Used by farm household	9	9	15	17	29	27
Off-farm work in days, 1939[b]	30	30	37	38	40	39

a Cropland excludes plowable pasture.
b Per farm operator.

TABLE 8

ECONOMIC AND FINANCIAL CHARACTERISTICS IN RELATION TO:

Farm Asset Size, 108 Counties Ranked in Three Groups
(dollar figures in thousands)

	ALL COUN-TIES	Large Size	Inter-mediate Size	Small Size	RATIO (%) OF "LARGE SIZE" TO ALL COUNTIES[b]
Economic Characteristics					
Physical assets per farm	$8.3	$15.5	$7.3	$4.1	187%
Physical assets in:					
Land	52%	57%	50%	49%	112%
Buildings	23	19	26	25	83
Non-real-estate	25	24	25	26	96
Cropland/total acreage[c]	40	46	42	33	115
Dwellings/farm real estate, 1930	16	11	18	20	69
Farm product value, 1939:					
Crops and livestock	63	75	60	54	119
Dairy products	13	12	15	13	92
Poultry and prod. and misc.	6	4	8	6	67
Used by farm household	18	9	17	27	50
Off-farm work in days, 1939[d]	35	30	38	39	86
Change in phys. asset value, 1930-1940	−22%	−21%	−23%	−22%	95%
Financial Characteristics					
Interest in physical assets of:					
Operators	48%	44%	50%	52%	92%
Landlords	29	34	28	25	117
Creditors	23	23	22	23	100
Mtgd. farms/all farms	43	48	43	37	112
Mtg. debt/value of mtgd. farms	40	39	42	39	97
Mtg. debt/value of all farms	19	20	19	16	105
Farm mtg. debt held by:					
FLB's and FFMC	47	45	45	51	96
Ins. and mtg. investment companies	12	19	11	6	158
Commercial and savings banks	10	7	10	12	70
Individuals and miscellaneous	31	29	34	31	94
Non-real-estate loans, as % of total non-real-estate farm assets, of:					
Banks and PCA's	13	14	12	13	108
FSA and ECFL Division of FCA	8	4	8	12	50

Column group header: GROUPS OF COUNTIES[a] (36 EACH) CONTAINING FARMS OF:

[a] Averages for county groups are unweighted, except for physical assets per farm, which is weighted by number of farms in each county.

(footnotes concluded on next page)

Footnotes to Table 8 (concluded)

b The percentages shown in this column permit comparisons of the 36 counties with "large size" farms within the 108-county sample as a whole. In Table 6 the relatives for each of the 9-county groups included in the "large size" groups in Table 8 are averaged, with the result that different methods of weighting are involved in the two tables. In view of the purpose for which the comparisons are made, either method of comparing these 36 counties with the sample as a whole produces satisfactory indicators of any differences that the data are capable of revealing.

c Cropland excludes plowable pasture.

d Per farm operator.

groups, and only a slight variation is evident in the extent of their dependence for mortgage credit on federal and federally sponsored agencies or on individuals and miscellaneous lenders. Similarly, in the degree to which non-real-estate credit is drawn from banks and PCA's, differences between farm-size groups of counties appear to be slight. It should be noted, however, that this rough similarity of averages as between large-farm and small-farm county groups does not necessarily signify similarity as regards individual counties or even individual farms of different size. Dissimilarities in farm financial organization between individual farms or individual counties that are comparable with respect to farm size may be traceable to dissimilarities in other farm economic characteristics which the particular basis of county classification used in Table 8 has not brought out.[9]

The main findings to be drawn from Tables 5 through 8 are that important differences in farm financial organization are fairly consistently related to farm asset size. This does not mean, of course, that there is a direct causal relationship linking the two. Nor does it exclude the possibility that other asset characteristics of agriculture may be influential in determining farm financial organization. The following section deals with such alternative factors, namely the kinds and relative importance of assets utilized in farm production.

Relation of Farm Asset Composition to Financial Organization

The results obtained when county groups are arranged according to the percentage of total physical assets that consists of land

[9] Because significant relationships may be obscured in group averages, it is insufficient to rely upon a single cross-tabulation of the data to reveal all pertinent relationships, and separate tabulations each based on a selected indicator of difference among counties in the nature of their agriculture are used. For presentation, an attempt has been made to choose those tabulations that bring out relationship not revealed by others. But because economic characteristics of agriculture are intercorrelated, some duplication is unavoidable.

(Table 9) supplement and modify in some respects the findings based on a size-of-farm grouping (Table 8). Counties in which land is most important as an asset exhibit a relatively high landlord interest in farm assets, while those in which land ranks lowest among farm physical assets are characterized by high equity investment by the farm operator. These facts make a reasonably strong case for the additional generalization that the importance of operator and landlord interests in farm assets is significantly related to the type of assets used in farm production and to the nature of farming operations.

Counties characterized by a high land component of physical farm assets differ also with respect to other financial characteristics from counties with a low land component of assets. They are high with respect to frequency of mortgage debt, but low with respect to the ratio of debt to value of mortgaged farms, so that their ratio of mortgage debt to value of all farms averages about the same as for the entire 108-county sample. They rank high with respect to importance of centralized credit agencies as sources of farm mortgage credit; also in the amount of non-real-estate credit obtained from banks and PCA's. It should be observed, however, that these counties are also characterized by larger-than-average farms. In fact, many of them are found also in the large-farm group in Table 8.[10]

The middle and low groups in Table 9 afford a chance to compare groups of counties that differ little with respect to average asset size of farm, but differ markedly as regards other dimensions of asset composition and nature of product. Thus, the group for which land is of medium importance among assets has a lower percentage of real estate assets in the farm dwelling, and a higher percentage of product value in crop and livestock sales, than the group with a low land component. The differences between these two groups in farm financial organization are like those found between the high and medium land component counties, which differ sharply with respect to farm asset size. This suggests that asset composition may have a relationship to financial organization of agriculture that is independent of asset size of farm.

The fact that the "middle" group contains a number of southern counties, and the "low" group a substantial number of northern counties, raises again the question of whether regional influences are an independent determinant of farm financial organization.

[10] But a number of large-scale dairy counties that are in the large asset-size group in Table 8 are not among the high land component counties of Table 9.

TABLE 9

ECONOMIC AND FINANCIAL CHARACTERISTICS IN RELATION TO:

Land Component of Physical Assets, 108 Counties

(dollar figures in thousands)

	COUNTIES GROUPED BY LAND COMPONENT OF PHYSICAL ASSETS[a]			RATIO (%) OF HIGH 36 COUNTIES TO ALL COUNTIES
	High 36 Counties	Middle 36 Counties	Low 36 Counties	
Economic Characteristics				
Physical assets per farm	$11.1	$6.5	$7.6	134%
Physical assets in:				
Land	66%	52%	38%	127%
Buildings	14	22	33	61
Non-real-estate	20	26	29	80
Cropland/total acreage[b]	45	34	42	113
Dwellings/farm real estate, 1930	10	16	22	63
Farm product value, 1939:				
Crops and livestock	77	65	47	122
Dairy products	6	8	25	46
Poultry and prod. and misc.	4	5	9	67
Used by farm household	13	22	18	72
Off-farm work in days, 1939[c]	32	33	42	91
Change in phys. asset value, 1930-1940[d]	−22%	−22%	−23%	100%
Financial Characteristics				
Interest in physical assets of:				
Operators	40%	48%	58%	83%
Landlords	37	29	20	128
Creditors	23	23	22	100
Mtgd. farms/all farms	47	38	44	109
Mtg. debt/value of mtgd. farms	37	40	44	93
Mtg. debt/value of all farms	19	18	19	100
Farm mtg. debt held by:				
FLB's and FFMC	50	47	43	106
Ins. and mtg. investment companies	21	11	6	175
Commercial and savings banks	5	11	13	50
Individuals and miscellaneous	24	31	38	77
Non-real-estate loans, as % of total non-real-estate farm assets, of:				
Banks and PCA's	16	13	10	123
FSA and ECFL Division of FCA	7	10	6	88

(footnotes on next page)

Footnotes to Table 9

ᵃ Group averages are unweighted, except for physical assets per farm, which is weighted by the number of farms in the several counties.

ᵇ Cropland excludes plowable pasture.

ᶜ Per farm operator.

ᵈ Counties are regrouped as explained in Chapter 2. When grouped from a direct array of the entire sample by percentage of assets in land, the difference between groups in average asset deflation is small, as can be seen from the following tabulation:

	High	Middle	Low
Change in physical asset value, 1930-1940	—24%	—21%	—22%
Physical assets in land	66	53	37

Little is gained, therefore, in this case by applying the analytical method designed to equalize asset deflation among the three groups of counties.

It should be noted, however, that the southern counties included in the middle group are characterized by relatively low-valued farms engaged heavily in crop production, while the northern counties in the low group are characterized by relatively small-scale general farming and dairying. The data so far developed are obviously not conclusive on this issue, and additional evidence will be introduced at later points.

But, regional influences apart, the fact of dissimilarity in types of agriculture as between the "middle" and "low" groups of counties provides at least a partial explanation of the observed differences in their farm financial organization. High operator interests in the "low" group may be partially due to a reluctance on the part of absentee landlords to invest in even moderate-sized farms with assets consisting so largely of buildings, livestock, and equipment. The operator, also, may derive some advantage by owning rather than renting if the farm operations use nonland assets extensively, particularly when many day-to-day decisions are to be made in adapting assets to his operations. He stands to gain from giving good care to these assets and by the exercise of better-than-average judgment in their selection and use. Moreover, the absentee supplier of capital, whether as owner or lender, may tend to restrict investment in such farms—dairying and general farming, for example—in order to limit the risks associated with farm operations in which management in contrast to weather and product prices is the crucial element in success.

However, regional institutional differences cannot be ignored; rental contracts and other tenure arrangements used in the southern counties, which often involve substantial control of operations by the landlord, may protect the landlord against loss to about the same extent as would a mortgage against the property of an owner operator in another region. The substantive content of mortgage and rental contracts may be more significant for interregional comparisons than the relationship between the operator and the supplier of capital.

Two additional comparative analyses (Table 10) may serve to clarify further the relationship between farm financial organization and the composition of farm assets.[11] The first is made by taking the 36 large-farm counties identified in Table 8, arraying them according to the percentage of physical assets in land, and placing the upper half of the array in a "high" group and the lower half in a "low" group. A comparison of the economic and financial characteristics of these two sets of eighteen counties makes it possible to study the relation between what may be called the land-asset component of farms and their financial organization, where the influence of farm size has been partially eliminated.

The large-farm counties with a relatively high proportion of assets in land are characterized by (1) low operator and high landlord interests, (2) comparatively high frequency of mortgage debt, (3) a low ratio of mortgage debt to the value of mortgaged farms, (4) low dependence on mortgage credit from banks and individuals, (5) high dependence on insurance company mortgage credit, (6) somewhat greater use of mortgage credit from the federal and federally sponsored credit agencies, and (7) relatively heavy use of non-real-estate credit.

The two large-farm county groups in Table 10 differ less in asset size of farm ($17,500 and $14,200 for the high and low land component counties respectively) than their combined average differed from the small-farm group in Table 8 ($15,500 versus $4,100). Yet in a number of respects the differences in their financial organization are more marked. For example, in Table 8 it is found that operator interest is 44 and 52 per cent, respectively, for the "large size" and "small size" groups. But when in Table 10 the "large size" group is subclassified according to importance of land in total assets, the operator interest is 37 per cent for the high land component group and 50 per cent for the low land component group. Furthermore, banks, individuals, and miscellaneous mortgage lenders held 36 and 43 per cent, respectively, of total mortgage debt in the "large size" and "small size"

---

[11] Relationships of asset composition to financial organization are so clearcut in Table 10 that little is added by further breakdowns within asset-deflation quartiles such as were shown for the relationships of asset size to financial organization.

groups of Table 8, but 24 and 48 per cent, respectively, of the high and low land component groups of Table 10.

Further evidence suggesting that asset composition and associated product characteristics of agriculture may be more influential than asset size in determining financial organization of agriculture can be adduced from a breakdown of the small size group in Table 8 similar to that presented for the large size group in Table 10. Selected items for that breakdown are shown below along with comparable items for the large-farm, low land component group of Table 10.

	Large Size, Low Land Component (18 Counties)	Small Size, High Land Component (18 Counties)
Physical assets per farm	$14,200	$4,000
Physical assets in land	47%	56%
Dairy products/value of products	19	·6
Interest in physical assets, of:		
Operators	50	45
Landlords	27	32
Mortgage debt held by banks, individuals, or miscellaneous lenders	48	37

The results illustrate the need to consider exceptions to the average pattern of relationships revealed by the summary tabulations. In this case it appears that influences stemming from other economic characteristics of the agriculture in the two groups of counties are sufficient to offset those that might be expected to stem exclusively from differences in asset size. The difference in the importance of dairy farming in the two groups (analyzed in the following chapter) may be a major factor offsetting the influence of asset size on financial organization.

In its second comparison, Table 10 takes the 36 counties identified in Table 9 as high group in the proportion of total physical assets in land, and from an array according to the percentage of acreage in cropland divides them equally into "high" and "low" groups. Thus it is possible to compare the financial characteristics of groups of counties similar as to the importance of land but differing with respect to kind of land. Although no data are available for 1940 on the relative value per acre of cropland and non-cropland, it is possible to derive indicators of the relative importance of cropland value in total assets in different groups of counties by assuming that value per acre is the same for each

TABLE 10

ECONOMIC AND FINANCIAL CHARACTERISTICS IN RELATION TO:

Land Component of Physical Assets and Cropland Component of Acreage, Two Groups of Counties

(dollar figures in thousands)

	36 LARGE-FARM COUNTIES GROUPED BY LAND COMPONENT OF PHYSICAL ASSETS[a]		36 HIGH LAND COMPONENT COUNTIES, GROUPED BY CROPLAND COMPONENT OF ACREAGE[a]	
	High 18 Counties	Low 18 Counties	High 18 Counties	Low 18 Counties
Economic Characteristics				
Physical assets per farm	$17.5	$14.2	$12.1	$9.9
Physical assets in:				
Land	68%	47%	67%	65%
Buildings	13	24	16	14
Non-real-estate	19	29	18	22
Cropland/total acreage[b]	48	42	60	26
Dwellings/farm real estate, 1930	9	14	11	10
Farm product value, 1939:				
Crops and livestock	84	66	80	74
Dairy products	5	19	5	7
Poultry and prod. and misc.	3	6	4	5
Used by farm household	8	10	11	14
Off-farm work in days, 1939[c]	29	30	21	42
Change in phys. assets value, 1930-1940	−18%	−23%	−23%	−21%
Financial Characteristics				
Interest in physical assets of:				
Operators	37%	50%	35%	44%
Landlords	40	27	41	34
Creditors	23	23	24	22
Mtgd. farms/all farms	51	44	51	43
Mtg. debt/value of mtgd. farms	34	42	39	34
Mtg. debt/value of all farms	20	21	21	16
Farm mtg. debt held by:				
FLB'S and FFMC	51	40	46	56
Ins. and mtg. investment companies	25	13	29	10
Commercial and savings banks	4	10	5	5
Individuals and miscellaneous	20	38	20	29
Non-real-estate loans, as % of total non-real-estate farm assets, of:				
Banks and PCA's	18	11	16	16
FSA and ECFL Division of FCA	5	3	7	7

(footnotes on next page)

Footnotes to Table 10

a Group averages are unweighted, except for physical assets per farm, which is weighted by the number of farms in the several counties.

b Cropland excludes plowable pasture.

c Per farm operator.

class of land. Thus for the two groups of counties in Table 10 it can be said that cropland value as a per cent of total assets differs by a ratio of about 40 to 17.

The two groups based on importance of cropland differ, but not greatly, with respect to asset size. They differ very sharply in importance of off-farm work of the operator. On the financial side, the high-cropland group is characterized by (1) relatively low operator and relatively high landlord interests, (2) both high mortgage debt frequency and high ratio of mortgage debt to value of mortgaged farms, and (3) relatively heavy use of insurance company mortgage credit. Banks, however, held about 5 per cent of the mortgage loans in both groups, whereas both the federally sponsored mortgage lenders and individuals held higher percentages in the low-cropland counties. A low cropland component of total assets appears to restrict landlord investment; also, total mortgage loans in relation to total real estate and the proportion of such loans held by private centralized lenders such as insurance companies are low in counties of this type.

Because individual county comparisons suggested an association between variations in the proportion of total asset value of farms represented by cropland value and variations in a bundle of other economic characteristics of agriculture which might be expected to have a similar influence on financial organization of farms, an analysis based on this factor is presented in greater detail in Chart 3. Here, since the comparisons are not limited to groups similar in the land component of assets, comparisons as to the importance of cropland have to be made in value terms rather than in acreage. The proportion of total assets represented by cropland was approximated for each county from the estimates of the proportion of total assets represented by land value and the percentage of acreage in cropland.[12] The counties were then grouped into 12 groups of 9 counties each, using the same method for equalizing asset deflation in the thirties as that described in Chapter 2. To facilitate graphic presentation, the data for the 12

[12] In these calculations value per acre for cropland and that for other land are assumed equal. The absolute percentages thus derived probably are too low, because value of cropland in individual counties would be expected to be higher per acre than value of other land. But used only for ranking, the percentages are adequate.

groups of counties are given as relatives based on the average for the entire 108 counties.

From Chart 3 it can be seen that as cropland increases as a component of total assets, landlord interests rise and operator interests fall. As in other comparisons based on economic characteristics of agriculture, the level of creditor interests does not appear to be closely related to the importance of cropland in total assets; but such relationship as there is appears to be the same as that for landlord interests. It can be seen also that in these three comparisons the two nine-county groups with lowest and highest cropland component of assets diverge from the relationships shown for the other ten groups of counties. Lowest cropland ratios are found in range livestock agriculture, in which this ratio probably is inappropriate to measure differences in assets that would influence investor attitudes. The reason for the divergence of counties with high crop ratios is not readily apparent, but with only nine counties in a group it is possible that sufficient influence is exerted by other characteristics of the agriculture to account for this divergence.

The chart reveals also a tendency for local lenders' proportion of mortgage loans to fall and centralized lenders' proportion to rise with increasing ratios of cropland to total asset values. However, any separate relationship between the cropland ratio and the proportion of mortgage loans held by federal land banks and the Federal Farm Mortgage Corporation is very slight.

In the interpretation of the relationships revealed by Chart 3 it is well to remember that the use of the ratio of cropland to total assets to classify counties also tends to classify counties by regions. Thus the groups with low-cropland ratios tend to be composed of counties located in the Northeast and the Mountain states, whereas the group with high-cropland ratios tends to reflect the grain areas and cash crop areas in the South. Despite this fact, it is significant for the evaluation of separate regional influences that even when these geographically different areas are combined for the purpose of this rather detailed grouping of counties, fairly consistent patterns of relationship still are obtained.

The other indicators of asset characteristics of agriculture used in the study are either directly related to, or are intercorrelated with, the asset characteristics already used as a basis of county classification. For example, grouping counties according to the land component of assets also effects a reasonably good classification according to the importance of all farm buildings and of

CHART 3

Selected Financial Characteristics Related to Percentages
of Assets in Cropland, 1940

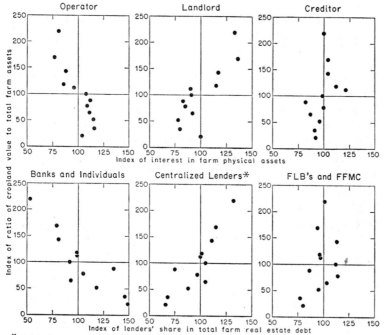

* Includes insurance and mortgage investment companies and the federally sponsored
mortgage credit agencies.

residential buildings, and the ratio of non-real-estate assets to total assets. Tabulations by the latter criteria do not add significantly to the results, and are not presented. The data presented so far also indicate that variations in the importance of particular asset characteristics are related to variations in other economic characteristics of agriculture reflected in product characteristics. Thus the one third of the counties characterized by a high non-real-estate component of assets are also high with respect to dairy products. But despite these intercorrelations, direct comparisons of county groups classified according to specific product characteristics yield additional insights. A selected group of such comparisons is presented in Chapter 4.

FARM PRODUCT CHARACTERISTICS IN RELATION TO THE FINANCIAL ORGANIZATION OF THE AGRICULTURE

THIS chapter presents a number of comparisons based on the types of output produced on the farms of the sample counties. In order to bring out the salient features of farm financial organization as they are related to different product-component patterns of agriculture, we have classified the 108 counties first into three primary groups—"high," "middle," and "low"—according to the percentage of the total value of farm output represented by product sales and by farm-home consumption. Second, within "high" groups, we have made further classifications designed to reveal relationships that are concealed in the group averages.

As has already been noted, the process of grouping counties according to specific asset characteristics tends to classify them also according to product characteristics. For this reason, some of the primary tabulations in the present chapter are discussed only briefly, and more attention is given to supplemental tabulations in which high "thirds" of the sample are analyzed in some detail.

Crop and Livestock Sales

In most significant respects, the evident differences between the counties that are "high," "middle," and "low" with regard to sales of crops and livestock resemble closely the differences revealed when counties are classified into three groups according to the land-to-asset ratio (Table 11).[1] The "high" 36 counties again include a large proportion of those with the biggest asset-size farms and those in which land is most important among all assets. On the financial side they are characterized by relatively low operator and relatively high landlord interests in assets. They have, moreover, a somewhat higher-than-average percentage of farms under mortgage and a somewhat lower-than-average ratio of mortgage debt to the value of mortgaged farms, although no sharp differentiation emerges on these points with either of the two bases of selection. Similarly, the counties that are found to be

[1] As indicated by previous tabulations, many of the counties that rank high on the one basis of classification rank high on the other as well.

high on the basis of crop and livestock sales draw relatively heavily on insurance companies for mortgage credit and use relatively more non-real-estate credit from commercial banks and PCA's.

It is apparent in Table 11 that substantial differences in financial organization are observable among farm counties that differ but little in the average asset size of their farms. The disparity between the "middle" and "low" counties in this respect may be due to the fact that these two groups differ sharply from one another in asset as well as in product composition. The "low" group has a substantially higher proportion of its farm assets in buildings and non-real-estate assets than the "middle" group, and a relatively higher proportion of the output of its farms in dairy, poultry, and miscellaneous products. These economic characteristics are associated with relatively high operator interest in assets and a high proportion of mortgage credit drawn from local sources.

When the 36 counties with the highest percentage of farm product value in crops and livestock are divided into two groups of 18 each according to the percentage of acreage in cropland, comparison can be made between the financial structures of predominantly large crop farm counties and those of predominantly large range livestock counties (Table 12). It will be observed that while the number of days of off-farm work per farm operator is twice as high in one group as in the other, differences are minor with respect to general indicators of asset size and composition of assets and products.

The principal contrast revealed by this table is to be noted in the financial characteristics. The "high-cropland" counties have relatively high landlord interests, high debt frequency, high debt-to-value ratios, and a heavy reliance on insurance companies as a source of long-term credit. The "low-cropland" counties, despite a farm asset size 50 per cent larger than that of the average for the entire sample ($8.3 thousand), obtained 37 per cent of all real estate credit from individuals and miscellaneous lenders as compared with 31 per cent for the entire 108 counties and 16 per cent for the high-cropland group of 18 counties. These low-cropland counties obtained relatively little real estate credit from insurance companies. Little difference is found, however, between the two groups of eighteen counties with respect to percentage of mortgage loans from commercial and savings banks and from the federally sponsored mortgage lenders; nor is there much dif-

TABLE 11

ECONOMIC AND FINANCIAL CHARACTERISTICS IN RELATION TO:

Percentage of Farm Product in Crop and Livestock, 108 Counties

(dollar figures in thousands)

	COUNTIES GROUPED BY PERCENTAGE OF PRODUCT VALUE IN CROP AND LIVESTOCK SALES[a]			RATIO (%) OF HIGH 36 COUNTIES TO ALL COUNTIES
	High 36	Middle 36	Low 36	
Economic Characteristics				
Physical assets per farm	$12.4	$6.9	$6.6	149%
Physical assets in:				
Land	63%	51%	43%	121%
Buildings	14	24	31	61
Non-real-estate	23	25	26	92
Cropland/total acreage[b]	38	45	37	95
Dwellings/farm real estate, 1930	10	17	22	62
Farm product value, 1939:				
Crops and livestock	83	63	43	132
Dairy products	4	12	23	31
Poultry and prod. and misc.	3	6	10	50
Used by farm household	10	19	24	56
Off-farm work in days, 1939[c]	30	32	44	86
Change in phys. asset value, 1930-1940[d]	−21%	−23%	−23%	95%
Financial Characteristics				
Interest in physical assets of:				
Operators	38%	48%	60%	79%
Landlords	39	27	20	134
Creditors	23	24	20	100
Mtgd. farms/all farms	45	43	40	105
Mtg. debt/value of mtgd. farms	37	42	41	92
Mtg. debt/value of all farms	19	18	18	100
Farm mtg. debt held by:				
FLB'S and FFMC	48	55	38	102
Ins. and mtg. investment companies	19	10	8	158
Commercial and savings banks	6	9	14	60
Individuals and miscellaneous	27	26	40	87
Non-real-estate loans, as % of total non-real-estate farm assets, of:				
Banks and PCA's	17	13	9	131
FSA and ECFL Division of FCA	6	11	6	75

(footnotes on next page)

Footnotes to Table 11

a Group averages are unweighted, except for physical assets per farm, which is weighted by the number of farms in the several counties.

b Cropland excludes plowable pasture.

c Per farm operator.

d Regrouping the counties to equalize average asset deflation in the 1930's serves mainly to place the "middle" and "low" groups on a more comparable basis with respect to financial indicators. The following data based on a straight array are included for purposes of comparison:

	High	Middle	Low
Per cent of product in crop and livestock sales	83	64	42
Percentage change in physical assets, 1930-1940	21	27	18

ference with respect to the importance of non-real-estate loans from banks and PCA's as compared with loans from direct federal lenders in the non-real-estate credit field.

The high-cropland counties in Table 12 thus represent a combination of characteristics which appears to attract equity investment by nonoperators and mortgage loans by private, centralized lenders such as insurance companies. High-cropland agriculture apparently can draw on a broader capital market for its financing than can the low-cropland group, which is heavily weighted with range livestock agriculture.[2]

Dairy Product Sales

We shall now seek to determine whether there are distinctive financial characteristics of agriculture in counties in which dairy product sales amount to a relatively high percentage of value of product. For this purpose we may group the 108 counties according to the percentage ratio of dairy product sales to total product value as of 1939 (Table 13). The fact that the 36 counties that are high in this respect include a number of small-scale dairy and general farm counties explains the somewhat lower-than-average asset size of farms in this group; but previous tabulations suggest that the difference in asset size cannot alone account for the marked differences in farm financial structure as between this and the other two groups. Outstanding among the financial char-

---

[2] Although landlord investment in farms does not necessarily mean that capital is drawn from long distances, high landlord interest in assets appears unlikely unless a substantial number of the owners are of the absentee type. Moreover, ownership by landlords who live in nearby towns or cities represents a broadening of capital sources as compared with equity financing by farm operators. This is a type of financing in which the provision of capital is at least partially divorced from day-to-day management, thus permitting investment by persons who are not interested in direct farm operation; these constitute a broader group than do persons who are interested in the operation of farms.

TABLE 12

Thirty-Six Counties with the Most Farm Product in Crops and Livestock, Grouped by Cropland Component of Acreage

(dollar figures in thousands)

	36 COUNTIES WITH HIGHEST PERCENTAGE OF CROP AND LIVESTOCK SALES, GROUPED BY THE CROPLAND COMPONENT OF ACREAGE[a]	
	High 18	Low 18
Economic Characteristics		
Physical assets per farm	$12.5	$12.3
Physical assets in:		
Land	66%	60%
Buildings	15	13
Non-real-estate	19	27
Cropland/total acreage[b]	62	15
Dwellings/farm real estate, 1930	11	9
Farm product value, 1939:		
Crops and livestock	83	82
Dairy products	4	5
Poultry and prod. and misc.	3	3
Used by farm household	11	10
Off-farm work in days, 1939[c]	20	40
Change in phys. asset value, 1930-1940	−18%	−23%
Financial Characteristics		
Interest in physical assets of:		
Operators	34%	43%
Landlords	42	35
Creditors	24	22
Mtgd. farms/all farms	50	40
Mtg. debt/value of mtgd. farms	39	35
Mtg. debt/value of all farms	20	17
Farm mtg. debt held by:		
FLB's and FFMC	47	50
Ins. and mtg. investment companies	31	7
Commercial and savings banks	6	6
Individuals and miscellaneous	16	37
Non-real-estate loans, as % of total non-real-estate farm assets, of:		
Banks and PCA's	17	17
FSA and ECFL Division of FCA	6	7

[a] Group averages are unweighted, except for physical assets, which is weighted by the number of farms in the several counties.

[b] Cropland excludes plowable pasture.

[c] Per farm operator.

TABLE 13

ECONOMIC AND FINANCIAL CHARACTERISTICS IN RELATION TO:

Percentage of Farm Product in Dairy Products, 108 Counties

(dollar figures in thousands)

	COUNTIES GROUPED BY PERCENTAGE OF PRODUCT VALUE IN DAIRY PRODUCT SALES[a]			RATIO (%) OF HIGH 36 COUNTIES TO ALL COUNTIES
	High 36	Middle 36	Low 36	
Economic Characteristics				
Physical assets per farm	$7.6	$8.3	$9.3	92%
Physical assets in:				
Land	41%	55%	60%	79%
Buildings	32	21	17	139
Non-real-estate	27	24	23	108
Cropland/total acreage[b]	42	40	39	105
Dwellings/farm real estate, 1930	22	15	13	137
Farm product value, 1939:				
Crops and livestock	46	65	78	73
Dairy products	27	10	3	208
Poultry and prod. and misc.	8	7	3	133
Used by farm household	19	18	16	106
Off-farm work in days, 1939[c]	41	34	29	117
Change in phys. asset value, 1930-1940[d]	−22%	−24%	−20%	100%
Financial Characteristics				
Interest in physical assets of:				
Operators	59%	48%	40%	123%
Landlords	20	29	37	69
Creditors	21	23	23	91
Mtgd. farms/all farms	44	41	44	102
Mtg. debt/value of mtgd. farms	43	40	37	107
Mtg. debt/value of all farms	19	18	18	100
Farm mtg. debt held by:				
FLB's and FFMC	44	50	48	94
Ins. and mtg. investment companies	7	11	20	58
Commercial and savings banks	12	9	7	120
Individuals and miscellaneous	37	30	25	119
Non-real-estate loans, as % of total non-real-estate farm assets, of:				
Banks and PCA's	9	15	15	69
FSA and ECFL Division of FCA	6	9	8	75

(footnotes on next page)

Footnotes to Table 13

ᵃ Group averages are unweighted, except for physical assets per farm, which is weighted by the number of farms in the several counties.

ᵇ Cropland excludes plowable pasture.

ᶜ Per farm operator.

ᵈ A comparison of groups of counties based on a straight array with those shown in the table can be made from the following tabulation:

	High	Middle	Low
Dairy sales as per cent of total product value	28	9	3
Percentage change in physical assets, 1930-1940	—21	—31	—14

acteristics of these "high" counties are the relatively heavy dependence on operator investment, the relatively low dependence on landlord investment, and, where long-term mortgage credit is used, a relatively greater reliance on banks, individuals, and miscellaneous lenders and a relatively lesser reliance on insurance and mortgage investment companies.

The table indicates also that mortgaged farms in the "high" dairy product group tended to be somewhat more heavily mortgaged than those in the "low" group, but that the first group made relatively slight use of non-real-estate credit. The explanation may lie partly in the necessity for substantial investment in dairy herd and other working capital in these counties; such non-real-estate assets would perhaps tend to be financed by loans secured by real estate. It is pertinent to note, in this connection, that almost 50 per cent of the mortgage credit used by these farms was supplied by local lenders.[3]

Broadly speaking, similar patterns of association between high dairy product output and farm financial organization are evident even when the high counties are compared, in groups as small as nine, with the average for the entire 27 counties in each asset-deflation quartile (Table 14). Greater consistency is found among the four groups with respect to operator and landlord interests and ratio of mortgage debt to the value of mortgaged farms than with respect to sources of mortgage credit. Likewise the relative level of combined bank and PCA loans is more consistent among the four quartiles than the relative level of emergency non-real-estate loans. However, the nine high dairy counties

[3] In general, such lenders might be expected to hold more loans secured by real estate that were made for purposes other than the purchase of real estate than would be held by lenders such as insurance companies and the federally sponsored lending agencies. Moreover, centralized lenders operating according to fairly uniform loan standards would be expected to relate their loans more directly to value of real estate than would local lenders, who are in closer contact with the farmer's operations.

TABLE 14

ECONOMIC AND FINANCIAL CHARACTERISTICS:

Nine Counties with the Most Farm Product in Dairy Products Compared with Quartile Groups of Counties Ranked by Asset Deflation

| | NINE COUNTIES WITH HIGHEST PERCENTAGE OF TOTAL VALUE OF PRODUCT IN DAIRY PRODUCT SALES (AVG. FOR RESPECTIVE QUARTILE GROUP = 100) | | | | |
| | Asset-Deflation Quartiles[a] | | | | AVERAGE OF QUARTILES |
	1st	2nd	3rd	4th	
Dairy product sales/total value of product, 1939	188	212	200	219	205
Physical assets per farm	84	76	106	79	86
Land/total assets	88	74	68	86	79
Cropland/total acreage[b]	111	113	93	100	106
Interest in physical assets of:					
Operators	119	109	124	127	120
Landlords	78	85	55	62	70
Creditors	93	96	96	91	94
Mtgd. farms/all farms	108	100	106	97	103
Mtg. debt/value of mtgd. farms	105	112	111	108	109
Farm mtg. debt held by:					
FLB's and FFMC	105	97	71	113	96
Ins. and mtg. investment companies	88	50	36	68	60
Commercial and savings banks	113	144	137	86	120
Individuals and miscellaneous	92	103	144	104	111
Non-real-estate loans, as % of total non-real-estate farm assets:					
Banks and PCA's	63	66	64	82	69
FSA and ECFL Division of FCA	105	77	34	81	75

[a] The 108 counties were arrayed by degree of asset deflation in the 1930's, from greatest to least, and divided into quartiles.

[b] Cropland excludes plowable pasture.

in each instance ranked higher with respect to per cent of mortgage loans held by banks, individuals, and miscellaneous lenders than with respect to per cent held by insurance and mortgage investment companies.

It will be useful to refer to the classification by product composition as presented in Table 13 to examine further the generalization, suggested by earlier tabulations, that while asset size of farm is firmly associated with the use of outside capital, it is a combination of asset and product composition that most strongly influences the sources from which this capital will be drawn. For this analysis the 36 counties with high dairy product sales have been divided into two groups of 18 each, according to their average farm asset size (Table 15). It will be observed that the large dairy farm counties depend more heavily than the small on outside funds, that is, on landlord and creditor investment, and that they show a distinctly higher frequency of mortgage indebtedness and a relatively high mortgage debt-to-value ratio.[4]

While large-scale and small-scale dairy farm counties differ sharply in the degree of their dependence on mortgage credit, the distribution of their mortgage debt among the principal lender groups shows no comparable divergence. In other words, the economic characteristics of dairy farming may condition the attitudes of different real estate lenders even with respect to farms of comparatively large asset size. Moreover, non-real-estate loans by both types of lenders tend to be low in relation to non-real-estate assets, regardless of differences in farm size. The somewhat greater dependence on emergency loan agencies on the part of the group characterized by large dairy farms probably reflects the relatively more unfavorable financial experience of these counties in the 1930's.

Although assets per farm doubtless affect the proportion of total capital supplied by operators, it seems probable that the nature of the farming operations also exerts an influence. This is suggested by the fact that operator interest in the 18 large-scale dairy counties in Table 15 is greater than the average for the entire sample, despite the substantially larger average size of farms in these 18 counties. This greater operator interest may reflect a reluctance on the part of landlords to invest in such farm enterprises; it may also indicate an awareness, on the part of owner operators, of the advantages of holding title to a farm even though it may be subject to heavy mortgage.

The two groups of 18 counties in Table 12 which represent large-crop farms and range livestock farms, respectively, may be compared with the 18 counties in Table 15 representing large-scale dairy farms. Selected items are assembled for ready comparison in the tabulation on the following page.

[4] The relatively high landlord and creditor interest in the group of large dairy farm counties may be due in part to the fact that they suffered a somewhat greater asset devaluation in the 1930's than the group of counties with smaller farms. These 36 counties have not been regrouped to equalize asset deflation for the two 18-county groups.

We have here three groups of 18 counties each that differ little with respect to average asset size of farm, but greatly with respect to asset and product composition and the general nature of their farming operations. Differences in operator and landlord

Economic and Financial Characteristics	Crop Farming[a] (18)	Range Livestock Farming[b] (18)	Large- Scale Dairy Farming[c] (18)
Physical assets per farm	$12.5	$12.3	$10.7
Interest in physical assets of:			
Operators	34%	43%	52%
Landlords	42	35	24
Creditors	24	22	24
Mtgd. farms/all farms	50	40	55
Mtg. debt/value of mtgd. farms	39	35	52
Farm mtg. debt held by:			
FLB's and FFMC	47	50	44
Ins. and mtg. investment companies	31	7	8
Commercial and savings banks	6	6	12
Individuals and miscellaneous	16	37	36
Non-real-estate loans as % total non-real-estate farm assets, of:			
Banks and PCA's	17	17	9
FSA and ECFL Division of FCA	6	7	7

[a] "High 18" counties in Table 12.
[b] "Low 18" counties in Table 12.
[c] "Large-scale" dairy counties in Table 15.

interests in assets are of the same order as those found between groups of counties arranged according to asset-size differences, but the three groups vary but slightly in total creditor interest. Both the "crop-farming" counties and the large-scale dairy counties show a greater use of mortgage credit than the range livestock counties. The low-cropland base may explain in part the lesser use of mortgage credit in the latter counties. Moreover, the higher incidence of mortgage credit in the dairy group, as compared with the crop-farming group, may reflect the financing practices characteristic of dairying, in which owner operation tends to prevail. Owner operators may do more of their financing with mortgage credit, even for non-real-estate assets, because they own the real estate that they operate. In the crop-farming counties the operator is less likely to own the real estate and would have to borrow on some other basis. Furthermore, landlords who do not also own the livestock and equipment could offer only the real estate as security for loans. For these reasons, differences in the

TABLE 15

ECONOMIC AND FINANCIAL CHARACTERISTICS:

Thirty-six Counties with the Most Farm Product in Dairy Products, Grouped by Farm Asset Size

(dollar figures in thousands)

	36 COUNTIES WITH HIGHEST PER CENT OF TOTAL VALUE OF PRODUCT IN DAIRY PRODUCT SALES, GROUPED BY FARM ASSET SIZE[a]	
	Large-Scale (18)	Small-Scale (18)
Economic Characteristics		
Physical assets per farm	$10.7	$4.6
Physical assets in:		
Land	42%	41%
Buildings	31	32
Non-real-estate	27	27
Cropland/total acreage[b]	51	34
Dwellings/ farm real estate, 1930	19	24
Farm product value, 1939:		
Crops and livestock	51	41
Dairy products	29	25
Poultry and prod. and misc.	8	9
Used by farm household	12	25
Off-farm work in days, 1939[c]	36	46
Change in phys. asset value, 1930-1940	−28%	−17%
Financial Characteristics		
Interest in physical assets of:		
Operators	52%	65%
Landlords	24	17
Creditors	24	18
Mtgd. farms/all farms	55	32
Mtg. debt/value of mtgd. farms	52	34
Mtg. debt/value of all farms	25	14
Farm mtg. debt held by:		
FLB's and FFMC	44	43
Ins. and mtg. investment companies	8	6
Commercial and savings banks	12	12
Individuals and miscellaneous	36	39
Non-real-estate loans, as % of total non-real-estate farm assets, of:		
Banks and PCA's	9	9
FSA and ECFL Division of FCA	7	5

[a] Group averages are unweighted, except for physical assets per farm, which is weighted by the number of farms in the several counties.

[b] Cropland excludes plowable pasture.

[c] Per farm operator.

use of real estate credit may also reflect underlying asset owner-ship patterns.

The data presented in Tables 10 to 15 enable us to compare the financial characteristics of large-scale crop farms and small-scale dairy farms, the former represented by the "high" 18 counties of Table 12 and the latter by the "low" 18 of Table 15. Selected indicators of financial organization for these two groups of counties are shown in the following tabulation.

Financial Characteristics	Large-Scale Crop Farm Counties (18)	Small-Scale Dairy Farm Counties (18)
Interests in physical assets of:		
Operators	34%	65%
Landlords	42	17
Creditors	24	18
Mtgd. farms/all farms	50	32
Mtg. debt/value of mtgd. farms	39	34
Mtg. debt/value of all farms	20	14
Mtg. debt held by lender groups:		
FLB's and FFMC	47	43
Ins. and mtg. investment companies	31	6
Commercial and savings banks	6	12
Individuals and miscellaneous	16	39
Non-real-estate loans, as % of total non-real-estate farm assets, of:		
Banks and PCA's	17	9
FSA and ECFL loans	6	5

It is clear from this comparison that the large-scale crop farms are financed heavily with outside equity funds, and by real estate creditors who lend over a broad area, while the small-scale dairy farms are financed to a much greater extent with the operator's own funds and by local sources of real estate credit. In contrast to most of the comparisons presented thus far, these two groups show a substantial difference in the creditor as well as the land-lord interest in assets. Two factors probably contribute to the moderate use of credit of both types in the small-scale dairy farm counties. First, many of these counties maintain an agriculture which provides a very poor base for ordinary business credit. In such counties the scale of operations is small and the proportion of total product available for sale is also small. Here, too, lending costs are likely to be high per $1,000 of loan value. Second, capital probably is of less importance in the total production process, as compared with labor, than in other kinds of agriculture. The average small-farm operator needs less capital to conduct his enterprise, with the result that a reduced demand for credit probably combines with high lending costs to cut down total credit use.

Farm-Home Consumption of Products

Because so-called "subsistence farming" is in some respects a distinct type of agriculture, it is relevant to consider whether it exhibits any distinctive financial characteristics. To this end the 108 counties are grouped in Table 16 according to the proportion of total farm product represented by home consumption. It will be noted that the counties in which home consumption is highest contain farms that are small in asset size and have a relatively low proportion of acreage in cropland. Further, the farm dwellings in these counties account for a relatively large proportion of farm real estate value, and the number of days of off-farm work is somewhat higher than that in other counties.

As would be expected, the financial characteristics of farms in the 36 counties that are highest with respect to home consumption of product are much like those of the counties that are low with respect to farm asset size: that is, they exhibit high operator and low landlord and creditor interest, accompanied by somewhat lower average frequency of mortgage debt and ratio of debt to value of mortgaged farms.[5] Compared with the counties most remote from them in character, the subsistence farming counties depend somewhat more heavily on commercial and savings banks and individuals for mortgage credit and draw on insurance company sources to a lesser extent. Little difference is to be observed, however, in the proportion of total loans held by the federally sponsored mortgage credit agencies; the percentage is about the same for counties where home consumption of farm products is high as for those in which it is least characteristic.

Although subsistence farming does, as we have seen, account for certain differences in financial characteristics, some of these differences are less marked than when other bases of classification are employed. For example, landlord and operator interests differ little as between the "high" and "middle" groups. It will be noted also that differences between these two groups with respect to asset patterns and product composition (other than farm-home consumption) are not especially pronounced. This suggests that the financial organization of agriculture may be related more

[5] Both 36-county groups contain a large proportion of the same counties.

TABLE 16

ECONOMIC AND FINANCIAL CHARACTERISTICS IN RELATION TO:

Percentage of Farm Product Consumed in Farm Homes, 108 Counties

(dollar figures in thousands)

	COUNTIES GROUPED BY PERCENTAGE OF FARM-HOME CONSUMPTION OF FARM PRODUCT[a]			RATIO (%) OF HIGH 36 COUNTIES TO ALL COUNTIES
	High 36	Middle 36	Low 36	
Economic Characteristics				
Physical assets per farm	$4.5	$7.4	$14.5	54%
Physical assets in:				
Land	50%	48%	58%	96%
Buildings	25	26	18	109
Non-real-estate	24	26	24	96
Cropland/total acreage[b]	34	44	44	85
Dwellings/farm real estate, 1930	20	18	12	125
Farm product value, 1939:				
Crops and livestock	52	60	78	82
Dairy products	13	17	10	100
Poultry and prod. and misc.	6	7	4	100
Used by farm household	29	16	8	161
Off-farm work in days, 1939[c]	41	34	31	117
Change in phys. asset value, 1930-1940[d]	−22%	−23%	−22%	100%
Financial Characteristics				
Interest in physical assets of:				
Operators	54%	49%	42%	113%
Landlords	26	27	34	90
Creditors	20	24	24	87
Mtgd. farms/all farms	37	43	49	86
Mtg. debt/value of mtgd. farms	38	42	40	95
Mtg. debt/value of all farms	16	19	20	84
Farm mtg. debt held by:				
FLB's and FFMC	48	44	47	102
Ins. and mtg. investment companies	9	12	17	75
Commercial and savings banks	12	10	7	120
Individuals and miscellaneous	31	34	29	100
Non-real-estate loans, as % of total non-real-estate farm assets, of:				
Banks and PCA's	12	12	15	92
FSA and ECFL Division of FCA	9	9	6	113

(footnotes on next page)

ᵃ Group averages are unweighted, except for physical assets per farm, which is weighted by the number of farms in the several counties.

ᵇ Cropland excludes plowable pasture.

ᶜ Per farm operator.

ᵈ For comparison with data presented in the table, the percentage of total value of product represented by farm-home consumption and the change in physical assets, 1930-1940, are shown below for three groups of counties based on a straight array without reference to asset change in the 1930's.

	High	Middle	Low
Home consumption as per cent of value of product	30	15	8
Percentage change in physical assets, 1930-1940	−14	−27	−25

directly to asset composition and product-sale patterns than to the home use of a farm's products.

When the "high" 36 subsistence farming counties are divided into two groups according to the importance of dairy products in total sales, the "high" 18 tend to consist mainly of small-scale general farm counties of the North, and the "low" 18 mainly of small-scale crop-farming counties of the South (Table 17). The two groups of counties probably are more nearly comparable with respect to average asset-size of farm unit than the difference between $5,100 and $3,800 would suggest. The "low" 18 are heavily weighted with southern counties in which all tenant-operated farms (but not cropper farms) are included in the computation of average asset-size of farm. Since one landlord may have several tenant-operated farms in a tract of land that is financed as one unit, the number of "agricultural units" from the viewpoint of financing tends to be less than the number of "farms" from the viewpoint of operations. The two groups of counties do, however, show differences in operator and landlord interests that are consistent with the variations in kinds of agriculture.

Aside from the financial indicators mentioned above, we find little difference in most of them. Although the data in Table 17 are inadequate for the purpose, it probably would be found that below a given size of farm, differences in nature of assets and production exert less influence on financial organization than among larger farms. As capital needs per farm fall, financing becomes less of a commercial operation and the impact of general capital market influences may not be so pronounced. But this is a hypothesis that cannot be tested adequately with the present data.

Off-Farm Work

When the 108-county sample is broken down into "thirds" according to the amount of off-farm work, it is found that the

TABLE 17

ECONOMIC AND FINANCIAL CHARACTERISTICS:

Thirty-six Counties with the Most Farm Product Consumed in Farm Homes, Grouped by Percentage of Farm Product in Dairy Products

(*dollar figures in thousands*)

	36 COUNTIES WITH THE HIGHEST PERCENTAGE OF FARM-HOME CONSUMPTION OF FARM PRODUCT GROUPED BY THE PERCENTAGE OF FARM PRODUCT VALUE IN DAIRY PRODUCT SALES[a]	
	High 18	Low 18
Economic Characteristics		
Physical assets per farm	$5.1	$3.8
Physical assets in:		
Land	48%	54%
Buildings	28	22
Non-real-estate	24	24
Cropland/total acreage[b]	36	31
Dwellings/farm real estate, 1930	20	19
Farm product value, 1939:		
Crops and livestock	46	59
Dairy products	20	5
Poultry and prod. and misc.	8	4
Used by farm household	26	32
Off-farm work in days, 1939[c]	44	38
Change in phys. asset value, 1939-1940	−25%	−18%
Financial Characteristics		
Interest in physical assets of:		
Operators	59%	49%
Landlords	21	30
Creditors	20	21
Mtgd. farms/all farms	39	36
Mtg. debt/value of mtgd. farms	39	37
Mtg. debt/value of all farms	17	16
Farm mtg. debt held by:		
FLB's and FFMC	47	49
Ins. and mtg. investment companies	10	9
Commercial and savings banks	10	13
Individuals and miscellaneous	33	29
Non-real-estate loans, as % of total non-real-estate farm assets, of:		
Banks and PCA's	11	13
FSA and ECFL Division of FCA	7	8

[a] Group averages are unweighted, except for physical assets per farm, which is weighted by the number of farms in the several counties.
[b] Cropland excludes plowable pasture.
[c] Per farm operator.

counties that are relatively high in this respect do not differ greatly from those that are low as regards average assets per farm or the distribution of assets and products (Table 18). They do, however, exhibit a relatively low cropland component in total acreage. On the financial side, operator interests are relatively high, in marked contrast to the investment levels of both landlords and creditors. The interests of the latter in real estate as well as non-real-estate assets appear to be low. This last observation probably reflects the relative unattractiveness of such farm properties as loan security when compared with commercial farms and distinctly urban residences. The fact that in the counties "high" in incidence of off-farm work a larger-than-average percentage of mortgage loans was held by individuals and miscellaneous investors also suggests that these properties fail to conform readily to the standards of large-scale private institutional lenders.[6]

A still closer approximation to a type of agriculture that is on the borderline of the agricultural economy is achieved when the counties with the highest proportion of off-farm work are divided according to the percentage of assets represented by the farm dwelling (Table 19). The counties that are highest in this last respect may be called small-scale, part-time farming counties, and may be compared with the "low" 18 in Table 17, which have been characterized as small-scale, crop-farming counties.

The small-scale, part-time farming counties again exhibit a predominance of operator financing, supplemented by credit from local sources and only moderate use of non-real-estate credit. As might be expected, landlord interests are higher in the small-scale crop-farming counties than they are in the part-time farming group. Small-scale crop-farming counties tended to draw more heavily than the part-time farming counties on public financing facilities for both long- and short-term credit, while the part-time farming counties were distinctly more dependent on local private credit sources.

The 18 "low" counties in Table 19, characterized by high off-farm work but a low residential component of real estate assets, includes a substantial number of range livestock counties. The group as a whole, therefore, has average economic and financial

---

[6] A low cropland component of assets may help to explain this lender distribution, since other tabulations reveal a tendency for centralized, institutional lenders to be most active where the proportion of cropland to acreage is high.

TABLE 18

ECONOMIC AND FINANCIAL CHARACTERISTICS IN RELATION TO:

Number of Days of Off-Farm Work per Farm Operator, 108 Counties

(*dollar figures in thousands*)

	COUNTIES GROUPED BY NUMBER OF DAYS OF OFF-FARM WORK PER FARM OPERATOR[a]			RATIO (%) OF HIGH 36 COUNTIES TO ALL COUNTIES
	High 36	Middle 36	Low 36	
Economic Characteristics				
Physical assets per farm	$7.6	$7.1	$10.0	92%
Physical assets in:				
Land	50%	51%	55%	96%
Buildings	25	24	21	109
Non-real-estate	25	25	24	100
Cropland/total acreage[b]	27	38	56	68
Dwellings/farm real estate, 1930	17	18	14	106
Farm product value, 1939:				
Crops and livestock	59	60	70	94
Dairy products	15	14	11	115
Poultry and prod. and misc.	8	6	5	133
Used by farm household	18	20	14	100
Off-farm work in days, 1939[c]	56	32	16	160
Change in phys. asset value, 1930-1940[d]	−21%	−23%	−22%	95%
Financial Characteristics				
Interest in physical assets of:				
Operators	56%	49%	40%	117%
Landlords	25	28	34	86
Creditors	19	23	26	83
Mtgd. farms/all farms	40	42	47	93
Mtg. debt/value of mtgd. farms	36	40	42	90
Mtg. debt/value of all farms	16	18	21	84
Farm mtg. debt held by:				
FLB's and FFMC	43	50	46	92
Ins. and mtg. investment companies	7	10	20	58
Commercial and savings banks	12	11	7	120
Individuals and miscellaneous	38	29	27	123
Non-real-estate loans, as % of total non-real-estate farm assets, of:				
Banks and PCA's	11	13	15	85
FSA and ECFL Division of FCA	5	11	7	63

(footnotes on next page)

Footnotes to Table 18

ª Group averages are unweighted, except for physical assets per farm, which is weighted by the number of farms in the several counties.

ᵇ Cropland excludes plowable pasture.

ᶜ Per farm operator.

ᵈ Comparable data for number of days of off-farm work in 1939 and asset change, 1930-1940, based on a straight array of the counties, are given below:

	High	Middle	Low
Off-farm work per farm operator (in days), 1939	58	33	16
Percentage change in physical assets, 1930-1940	—19	—26	—22

characteristics similar to those of the 18 "low" counties of Table 12, which are still more heavily weighted with this type of agriculture. The composition of these 18 counties indicates that off-farm work is not sufficiently well correlated with other economic characteristics of agriculture to provide a clear-cut differentiation of patterns of farm financing.

General Observations

The comparisons presented thus far serve mainly to identify broad patterns of relationships between the financial organization of agriculture and its economic characteristics. The data set forth in this and the preceding chapter suggest fairly clear patterns of association between asset and product characteristics, on the one hand, and the extent of dependence on operator and landlord investment, on the other. They do not, however, indicate that the use of farm credit varies consistently with differences in farm assets and products. The lack of correspondence among groups of counties with respect to the relative importance of real estate and non-real-estate credit suggests that variations in farm credit use and in the terms on which credit is acquired by farms may be very great—so great, indeed, that creditor interest may be too heterogeneous to be meaningful.

The classifications in this and in earlier chapters indicate that certain characteristics of agriculture are associated with varying levels of activity on the part of particular lender groups. Such evidence as has been adduced, however, is largely a by-product of the grouping of counties by major asset and product classifications. This indirect method of analysis does not appear to be best adapted to a study of those agricultural patterns that are associated with high and low creditor interests as such, or of those in which different kinds of credit appear to be used more or less

86

TABLE 19

ECONOMIC AND FINANCIAL CHARACTERISTICS:

Thirty-six Counties with Most Off-Farm Work per Farm Operator, Grouped by Importance of Farm Dwelling in Total Farm Real Estate Value

(dollar figures in thousands)

	36 COUNTIES WITH MOST OFF-FARM WORK PER FARM OPERATOR, GROUPED BY IMPORTANCE OF FARM DWELLING IN TOTAL FARM REAL ESTATE VALUE[a]	
	High 18	Low 18
Economic Characteristics		
Physical assets per farm	$6.4	$10.1
Physical assets in:		
Land	38%	61%
Buildings	36	14
Non-real-estate	26	25
Cropland/total acreage[b]	35	19
Dwellings/farm real estate, 1930	25	9
Farm product value, 1939:		
Crops and livestock	55	72
Dairy products	23	9
Poultry and prod. and misc.	11	5
Used by farm household	21	14
Off-farm work in days, 1939[c]	62	52
Change in phys. asset value, 1930-1940	−18%	−24%
Financial Characteristics		
Interest in physical assets of:		
Operators	64%	50%
Landlords	18	30
Creditors	18	20
Mtgd. farms/all farms	41	39
Mtg. debt/value of mtgd. farms	36	36
Mtg. debt/value of all farms	16	16
Farm mtg. debt held by:		
FLB's and FFMC	34	49
Ins. and mtg. investment companies	6	8
Commercial and savings banks	18	6
Individuals and miscellaneous	42	37
Non-real-estate loans, as % of total non-real-estate farm assets, of:		
Banks and PCA's	9	13
FSA and ECFL Division of FCA	4	7

[a] Group averages are unweighted, except for physical assets per farm, which is weighted by the number of farms in the several counties.
[b] Cropland excludes plowable pasture.
[c] Per farm operator.

extensively in the capital structure of agriculture. In order to explore further the ways in which creditor participation may be related to various aspects of farm economic organization, we shall, in the two following chapters, proceed with the analysis of our 108-county sample by classifying counties according to selected indicators of farm credit use.

CHAPTER 5

RELATIONSHIPS OF CREDIT USE TO
ECONOMIC CHARACTERISTICS
OF THE AGRICULTURE

ALTHOUGH few clear-cut relationships between farm credit use and the economic characteristics of agriculture emerge when these aspects are examined separately, this does not mean that credit use is uninfluenced by the economic nature of agriculture. It is possible, rather, that certain clusters of agricultural characteristics, and not single economic factors, influence credit needs and lender attitudes. Moreover, single economic characteristics, or combinations of them, may have decisive effects on the use of particular kinds of credit even when their influence on the totality of farm credit cannot be established. It is toward an analysis of this possibility that the study will now be directed.

Data are given in Table 20 for eight counties—four in which there was very little use of credit, and four in which considerable credit was employed.[1] The four counties with low creditor interest represent widely different types of agriculture: Adams, a large-scale wheat county in Washington; Calvert, a small-scale tobacco and general farming county in eastern Maryland; Webb, a Texas range livestock county; and Blount, a county in the mountainous section of eastern Tennessee. Two of these—Adams and Webb—are characterized by large farms, the other two—Calvert and Blount—by farms that are smaller than average; in all other respects the economic characteristics of the four counties are widely dissimilar.

The relatively moderate use of credit in these four counties may be due in part, of course, to an unwillingness of lenders to place funds at the disposal of farmers engaged in a particular type of agriculture; and it may reflect also a lack of demand for credit funds either because little outside capital is required or

---

[1] The possibility that errors may be present in the estimates of the indicators of economic and financial characteristics of individual counties renders somewhat hazardous any attempt to explain differences in farm credit use by comparing the economic characteristics of the agriculture of counties in which the creditor interest is light with those of counties in which it is relatively heavy. But this risk may be overcome in large part if we select counties in which contrasts are sharp and for which the estimates conform in general with our understanding of the type of agriculture involved.

TABLE 20

ECONOMIC AND FINANCIAL CHARACTERISTICS IN RELATION TO:

Creditor Interest in Physical Assets, 8 Counties

(dollar figures in thousands)

| | CREDITOR INTEREST IN PHYSICAL ASSETS | | | | | | | |
| | Low Creditor Interest Counties | | | | High Creditor Interest Counties | | | |
	Adams, Wash.	Calvert, Md.	Webb, Tex.	Blount, Tenn.	Coahoma, Miss.	Greene, Ga.	Hamilton, Iowa	Bradley, Ark.
Creditor interest in phys. assets	15%	13%	13%	10%	30%	34%	33%	31%
Economic Characteristics								
Physical assets per farm	$39.1	$6.3	$37.9	$4.6	$24.4	$2.4	$22.6	$2.3
Physical assets in:								
Land	74%	40%	75%	53%	69%	44%	60%	49%
Buildings	8	45	4	28	17	28	20	24
Non-real-estate	18	15	21	19	14	28	19	27
Cropland/total acreage[a]	72	19	3	34	71	29	75	35
Dwellings/farm real estate, 1930	6	29	3	17	16	32	10	26
Farm product value, 1939:								
Crops and livestock	93	82	94	38	89	48	82	61
Dairy products	1	.....	4	15	1	6	6	3
Poultry and prod. and misc.	3	3	.....	6	.....	2	6	2
Used by farm household	3	15	2	41	10	44	6	34
Off-farm work in days, 1939[b]	16	45	48	68	11	26	14	32
Change in phys. asset value, 1930-1940	—8%	—15%	—3%	—2%	—9%	—6%	—32%	—26%

(concluded on next page)

TABLE 20 (concluded)

| | CREDITOR INTEREST IN PHYSICAL ASSETS | | | | | | | |
| | Low Creditor Interest Counties | | | | High Creditor Interest Counties | | | |
Financial Characteristics	Adams, Wash.	Calvert, Md.	Webb, Tex.	Blount, Tenn.	Coahoma, Miss.	Greene, Ga.	Hamilton, Iowa	Bradley, Ark.
Interest in physical assets of:								
Operators	46%	48%	41%	74%	23%	38%	34%	55%
Landlords	39	39	46	16	47	28	33	14
Creditors	15	13	13	10	30	34	33	31
Mtgd. farms/all farms	47	34	27	28	65	33	57	47
Mtg. debt/value of mtgd. farms	28	23	14	36	37	35	50	38
Mtg. debt/value of all farms	14	11	11	11	28	15	30	16
Farm mtg. debt held by:								
FLB's and FFMC	57	18	27	18	21	47	33	50
Ins. and mtg. investment companies	21	....	27	27	50	5	43	6
Commercial and savings banks	....	27	....	9	4	15	7	19
Individuals and miscellaneous	22	55	73	46	25	33	17	25
Non-real-estate loans as % of total non-real-estate farm assets, of:								
Banks and PCA's	9	11	8	3	25	12	26	25
FSA and ECFL Division of FCA	4	4	....	....	1	55	1	18

a Cropland excludes plowable pasture.　　ᵇ Per farm operator.

91

because the need is being met by some form of equity financing. In three of the counties, for example—Adams, Calvert, and Webb —landlord interests were substantially higher than the average for the entire sample (about 29 per cent), but in the fourth county—Blount—landlord interests were only 16 per cent; in this county of small farms there may have been little need for outside capital and not much to attract the investor of debt funds.

It should, perhaps, not be too surprising to find low creditor interests in large commercial farming counties, where capital requirements, particularly for real estate ownership, are met largely by landlords, and, at the same time, in small-scale subsistence agriculture, in which lenders would find security inadequate for the extension of credit.[2] That Calvert County belongs in neither of these categories suggests that still other economic factors— e.g. its location near two large cities—may account for its heavy landlord investment and restricted use of credit.

As for the four counties in which reliance on debt funds is relatively heavy, they also represent widely different types of agriculture: Coahoma, a delta county in Mississippi; Greene, a small-scale farming county in the poorer land area of Georgia; Hamilton, a large-scale farming county in North Central Iowa; and Bradley, a small-scale subsistence farming county in Arkansas. The two large-scale farming counties, Coahoma and Hamilton, are noteworthy for their extensive use of real estate credit, and the two small-scale farming counties, Greene and Bradley, for their use of the non-real-estate credit, particularly of the emergency type. The indebtedness of these small-scale farming counties consisted in 1940 largely of an accumulation of emergency and special purpose loans made by government agencies. Thus their high credit ratios may reflect the policy of public lending agencies during the depression years toward particular kinds of agriculture. But to the extent that Farm Security Administration and emergency crop and feed loans were substituted for credit that would have been obtained in the 1930's from merchants and other local sources if it had been available, the comparatively heavy reliance on debt funds may be indicative also of a continuing characteristic of the agriculture in these two counties.[3]

[2] An intensive study of each of these four counties probably would indicate specific reasons to account for moderate credit use. Detailed case studies, however, are beyond the scope of this work.

[3] It should be repeated that estimates of specific indicators of financial organization for the eight counties may contain substantial errors. Nevertheless, it is likely that Adams County, Washington, would fall at or near the

Whereas the data in Table 20 show wide variations in the economic characteristics as between the two sets of four counties, comparable averages for three 36-county groups in Table 21 reveal little variation from one third of the sample to another. The only respect in which the three groups differ markedly is the extent of off-farm work. Apparently, marked differences within groups of counties average out to about the same level in each of the three groups. This appears to be true even when the indicators are applied to the 108 sample counties arrayed in asset-deflation quartiles.

A partial explanation of the failure of Table 21 to reveal significant relationships between creditor interest and the several indicators of the economic nature of agriculture may be found in certain peculiarities of the data. For one thing, because of inadequate information on non-real-estate loans held by lenders other than the four specified types of lending institutions, the estimates for these miscellaneous lenders are necessarily rough approximations. A few of the counties may therefore be improperly classified among the three creditor interest groups. A second defect arises from the inclusion in the farm debt total of emergency and special purpose loans by governmental agencies. Some of the counties fall in the "high 36" group mainly because of large amounts of such loans, although the procedure whereby counties are regrouped to hold average financial experience in the 1930's relatively constant tends to reduce the influence of this factor. It is believed, however, that despite these deficiencies of the data, the three groups of counties differ sufficiently with respect to creditor interest to permit identification of any marked differences in the agriculture of these groups.

The lack of marked differences in Table 21 with respect to the nature of the agriculture may perhaps be attributed to deficiencies in the group averages. As a test of this possibility, each of the three groups was further distributed according to farm asset size and other criteria. Two of these frequency distributions—by ratio of land value to total assets and by ratio of cropland to total acreage—reveal differences between the "high" and "low"

---

lower end of an array based on true estimates and that Coahoma County, Mississippi, would fall at or near the upper end. Parenthetically, if these eight counties are representative of the whole sample, it may be understood why averages for county groups based on classifications according to specific indicators of asset and product characteristics do not show significant differences in the extent of creditor interests.

TABLE 21

ECONOMIC AND FINANCIAL CHARACTERISTICS IN RELATION TO:

Creditor Interest in Physical Assets, 108 Counties

(dollar figures in thousands)

	COUNTY GROUPS BY CREDITOR INTEREST IN PHYSICAL ASSETS			RATIO (%) OF HIGH 36 COUNTIES TO ALL COUNTIES
	High 36	Middle 36	Low 36	
Creditor interest in phys. assets	30%	22%	16%	130%
Economic Characteristics				
Physical assets per farm	$8.4	$8.8	$7.7	101%
Physical assets in:				
Land	53%	50%	52%	102%
Buildings	21	25	24	91
Non-real-estate	26	25	24	104
Cropland/total acreage[a]	42	42	37	105
Dwellings/farm real estate, 1930	16	16	17	100
Farm product value, 1939:				
Crops and livestock	67	62	61	106
Dairy products	10	17	12	77
Poultry and prod. and misc.	5	6	8	83
Used by farm household	18	15	19	100
Off-farm work in days, 1939[b]	26	37	43	74
Change in phys. asset value, 1930-1940[c]	−24%	−22%	−20%	109%
Financial Characteristics				
Interest in physical assets of:				
Operators	41%	50%	55%	85%
Landlords	29	28	29	100
Creditors	30	22	16	130
Mtgd. farms/all farms	47	45	37	109
Mtg. debt/value of mtgd. farms	43	41	36	108
Mtg. debt/value of all farms	21	19	15	110
Farm mtg. debt held by:				
FLB's and FFMC	54	41	44	115
Ins. and mtg. investment companies	10	16	12	83
Commercial and savings banks	8	11	10	80
Individuals and miscellaneous	28	32	34	90
Non-real-estate loans, as % of total non-real-estate farm assets, of:				
Banks and PCA's	19	12	18	146
FSA and ECFL Division of FCA	15	5	4	188

(footnotes on next page)

Footnotes to Table 21

a Cropland excludes plowable pasture.

b Per farm operator.

c Data on creditor interest in physical assets and change in physical assets, 1930-1940, based on a straight array, are shown below:

	High	Middle	Low
Creditor interest in physical assets	31%	22%	15%
Change in physical asset value, 1930-1940	−31	−21	−14

36 counties that may provide a partial explanation of differences in creditor interest, as follows:

	COUNTY GROUPS BY CREDITOR IN- TEREST IN PHYSICAL ASSETS	
	High 36	Low 36
Ratio of Land Value to Total Physical Assets		
Less than 40.0%	4	8
40.0 - 59.9	23	16
60.0 and over	9	12
Total counties	36	36
Ratio of Cropland to Total Acreage		
Less than 20.0%	10	15
20.0 - 49.9	15	7
50.0 and over	11	14
Total counties	36	36

In both frequency distributions the low group shows less concentration around the mean than the high group. This corroborates an impression gained from the study of individual counties, namely that low creditor interests are found in rather extreme kinds of agriculture. Agriculture with a low land component of assets and a low cropland component of acreage may exhibit a low creditor interest partly because creditors—particularly real estate lenders—find investment in such agriculture relatively unattractive. Counties that rank high in ratio of land value to total assets and ratio of cropland to total acreage may exhibit a low creditor interest for a different reason. Their agriculture may be so attractive to equity investment by nonoperators that less credit is needed in relation to total assets.

One hypothesis suggested by these data is that low creditor interest may be found both in the best agriculture—viewed from the standpoint of equity investment by nonoperators—and in the poorest—viewed from the standpoint of both creditor and equity investment by nonoperators. A second is that high creditor interest may occur in agriculture that does not meet all of the requirements of maximum equity investment by nonoperators but provides adequate security to creditors.

Influences other than those mentioned above doubtless are present in the determination of the creditor interest in different kinds of agriculture. Both the ability and the desire of owner operators to invest equity funds in farming must be related to the need for outside capital. Furthermore, creditors include lenders who react differently to different cost and risk situations; and needs for different kinds of credit vary with the nature of farming operations. The creditor interest thus may reflect such diverse elements, both of "capital supply" and of "capital need," that only a very general analysis of its relation to the economic nature of agriculture is warranted. This problem will be treated further when we come to consider real estate and non-real-estate credit and the importance of different sources of credit.

Creditor Interest in Relation to Total Outside Interest in Farm Physical Assets

It has already been suggested that differences among counties in the extent to which the outside interest in assets is represented by debt may be related to the economic characteristics of their agriculture.[4] In order to examine this hypothesis more closely, we have grouped the 108 counties first according to the ratio of outside interests to total physical assets. The 36 counties that are "high," and the 36 that are "low," are then divided into two groups of 18 each according to the ratio of creditor to total outside interest in physical assets. It thus becomes possible to contrast counties that are roughly alike as regards the percentage of outside interest in assets, but differ significantly in the extent to which this interest is held by creditors.

Among the counties with the greatest outside (or nonoperator) interest in farm assets, those that make the most extensive use of credit are characterized by relatively lower assets per farm, less emphasis on crops and livestock as a source of income, greater emphasis on dairying, greater use of products in home consumption, and more off-farm work. Differences between the two groups with respect to average asset composition are minor.

As asset size of farm for the high 18 counties in this comparison

---

[4] Outside interest is defined as all interests in assets except that of the operator.

is only slightly greater than for the 108-county sample as a whole, it will be instructive to compare this subgroup of 18 counties with the entire sample. Selected comparisons are set forth below:

	108 Counties	18-County Subgroup
Interests in physical assets of:		
Operators	48%	37%
Landlords	29	33
Creditors	23	30
Physical assets per farm	$8,300	$8,900
Physical assets in:		
Land	52%	60%
Buildings	23	17
Non-real-estate assets	25	23
Cropland/total acreage[a]	40	45
Dwellings/farm real estate	16	13
Farm product value, 1939		
Crops and livestock	63	69
Dairy products	13	10
Poultry and prod. and misc.	6	4
Used by farm household	18	17
Off-farm work in days, 1939[b]	35	30

[a] Cropland excludes plowable pasture.
[b] Per farm operator.

The 18-county subgroup employs a higher percentage of both landlord and creditor funds than the total of 108 counties, but the difference is greater for the creditor interests. Somewhat larger-than-average asset size of farm would be expected to effect a greater reliance on nonoperator sources of funds, but it would not explain the substantially heavier use of debt funds. An examination of the above comparisons does, however, suggest a partial explanation. In terms of the relationships of landlord interest to the economic characteristics of agriculture, the 18-county subgroup would appear to be somewhat more attractive to landlord investment than the average county in the entire sample. But it is possible that an agriculture is satisfactory for substantially greater-than-average use of credit even when it has characteristics that discourage outright equity investment by landlords. The terms of the loan contract can be adapted to permit higher loan ratios on real estate, whereas such adaptations are not possible in the case of outright ownership by nonoperators as a method of investment. The 18-county subgroup reveals also a higher proportion of farms under mortgage as well as a greater use of non-real-estate credit, as compared with the 108-county sample. The data do not, however, indicate why farmers and farm owners in the 18-county subgroup have a greater propensity to borrow. They merely help to corroborate the hypothesis, presented earlier in this chapter, that high credit use may be characteristic of an intermediate type of agriculture which is adequate as security for substantial amounts of loans but which, for particular reasons, may not be especially attractive to landlord investment.

It will be noted in Table 22 that in the comparison based on ratio of creditor to outside interests, the low group of 18 counties contains agriculture that would appear to be attractive as security for loans. Yet creditor interest in this group is the same as for the 108-county sample as a whole. The additional capital from outside sources needed to finance this agriculture apparently can be obtained to a considerable extent from nonoperators as equity investors; this may explain why creditors in this group account for no more funds than do creditors in the average county of the entire sample.

Among the 36 counties with the least outside interest in assets, those that make the most extensive use of credit are counties whose farms are characterized by (1) a low land component of assets, (2) a comparatively high percentage of non-real-estate assets, and (3) a high percentage of income from sales of dairy products. These data suggest again that debt funds are relatively important in agriculture that provides adequate security for credit but lacks those characteristics that attract appreciable landlord investment. The asset and product pattern of this agriculture may also be such that farm operators would prefer to own their properties, even though their equity funds must be supplemented by substantial amounts of debt capital, than to occupy a tenant status with moderate debts. Greater emphasis on dairy production and greater importance of buildings and non-real-estate assets may well require more freedom to make detailed day-to-day managerial decisions than is called for in the sort of agriculture where operations are more standardized and assets consist largely of land. The principles on which these managerial decisions are to be made may be much more difficult to incorporate into a lease than in the case of agriculture that emphasizes staple crop production.

From Table 22 we learn also that of the 36 counties least dependent on outside funds, the 18 that relied most on debt funds obtained 42 per cent of their mortgage credit from individuals and miscellaneous lenders, as compared with 31 per cent for the other 18 counties in this group. This finding may shed some light on differences in agriculture that account for varying proportions of creditor and landlord interests. In the counties with the higher creditor ratios, individual investors may have required mortgage security to protect their investments, whereas in the counties with the higher landlord interests they may have been willing to invest through outright ownership. The difference in financial organization of these two groups of counties may be more in the legal basis of investment of particular groups than in the groups providing capital for agriculture.

A further analysis of farm credit use is possible when, after dividing the 108-county sample into asset-deflation quartiles, we array each group of 27 counties independently according to the credit ratios of farms. In each asset-deflation quartile the nine counties having the highest creditor component of total outside interests in physical assets are singled out for comparison with the average of all 27 counties in that quartile. From these comparisons, which ignore the level of total outside financing, it appears that a high credit component of total outside interests is associated with smaller-than-average farms in which the land component of total assets is low and dairy and general farming are more important than in the average for the quartile. In this kind of agriculture, owner operators are usually responsible, either directly or indirectly, for providing a larger-than-average proportion of total capital. The high ratio of creditor to outside interest, therefore, reflects both an absolutely low contribution by landlords and a need on the part of owner operators to borrow to supplement their own funds.

Although the comparisons of the findings presented in Table 22 suggest some of the reasons why total creditor interest may be high or low in relation to total outside interests, the arrangement of the counties still groups together those with quite different patterns of credit and equity capital use. A county will appear in the high-credit-use classification regardless of which kind of creditor interest is large. Counties with very high real estate debt but low non-real-estate debt, others with moderately high debt levels of both kinds, and still others with low real estate debt but very high non-real-estate debt, all fall into the subgroup with a high ratio of credit to total outside interests. Further analysis is required, therefore, to discover what economic characteristics of farming are associated with different types of credit financing.

TABLE 22

ECONOMIC AND FINANCIAL CHARACTERISTICS IN RELATION TO:

Ratio of Creditor to Outside Interest in Physical Assets, 72 Counties

(dollar figures in thousands)

	COUNTIES GROUPED BY OUTSIDE INTEREST IN PHYSICAL ASSETS			
	High 36 Counties[a]		Low 36 Counties[a]	
	High 18 by Creditor/ Outside Interest	Low 18 by Creditor/ Outside Interest	High 18 by Creditor/ Outside Interest	Low 18 by Creditor/ Outside Interest
Creditor interest/outside interest in physical assets	47%	35%	60%	45%
Economic Characteristics				
Physical assets per farm	$8.9	$11.8	$6.7	$6.0
Physical assets in:				
Land	60%	61%	39%	46%
Buildings	17	15	33	30
Non-real-estate	23	24	28	24
Cropland/total acreage[b]	45	47	35	36
Dwellings/farm real estate, 1930	13	11	23	20
Farm product value, 1939:				
Crops and livestock	69	83	44	51
Dairy products	10	4	28	18
Poultry and prod. and misc.	4	3	10	9
Used by farm household	17	11	18	22
Off-farm work in days, 1939[c]	30	26	49	49
Change in phys. asset value, 1930-1940[d]	−23%	−23%	−22%	−21%
Financial Characteristics				
Interest in physical assets of:				
Operators	37%	34%	65%	61%
Landlords	33	43	14	22
Creditors	30	23	21	17
Mtgd. farms/all farms	50	43	45	38
Mtg. debt/value of mtgd. farms	43	39	42	40
Mtg. debt/value of all farms	22	20	19	16
Farm mtg. debt held by:				
FLB's and FFMC	54	50	41	45
Ins. and mtg. investment companies	13	21	5	12
Commercial and savings banks	7	5	12	12
Individuals and miscellaneous	26	25	42	31
Non-real-estate loans, as % of total non-real-estate farm assets, of:				
Banks and PCA's	22	13	10	8
FSA and ECFL Division of FCA	15	7	4	3

(footnotes on next page)

Footnotes to Table 22

ᵃ Each 36-county group is stratified by asset change in the 1930's when divided into eighteen-county groups.

ᵇ Cropland excludes plowable pasture.

ᶜ Per farm operator.

ᵈ Data on outside interest and asset change, 1930-1940, based on a straight array of the counties, are shown below:

	High	Middle	Low
Outside interest in physical assets	67%	52%	36%
Change in physical assets, 1930-1940	−31	−14	−21

Mortgage Holders' Interests in Farm Real Estate Assets

In Table 23 the sample has been broken down into three groups ranked as "high," "middle," and "low," in terms of the ratio of real estate loans to total real estate assets. From these data it appears that the counties with the highest ratios have relatively large farms with a comparatively high percentage of cropland, and are characterized also by low consumption of farm products and a relatively low incidence of off-farm work. These characteristics are certainly typical of an agriculture into which outside investment would be expected to flow rather more readily. But they fail to indicate why a greater-than-average proportion of this outside investment should take the form of real estate credit rather than of additional equity investment on the part of landlords.

With assets per farm in the high real-estate-debt counties more than $2,000 above the average for the entire sample, one might expect the proportion of capital furnished by the operators to be somewhat lower than average. The percentage is moderately lower than that for the sample as a whole, but in this group operators actually contributed about $4,600 on the average, as compared with about $4,000 for operators in all 108 counties. Although landlords in the high real-estate-debt counties contributed about the same proportion of total funds as landlords averaged in the entire sample—around 29 per cent—and although this again was larger in dollar amount than average landlord investment for all 108 counties, it was not enough larger to compensate for the disproportionately lower level of operator investment. Real estate credit appears to have made up for the deficiency in equity capital supply for this group of counties: both the proportion of farms under mortgage and the ratio of debt to value of mortgaged farms were well above the average.[5] A part

⁵ High real estate credit may, of course, represent borrowing on real estate rather than on non-real-estate security. But in this case there appears to be

TABLE 23

ECONOMIC AND FINANCIAL CHARACTERISTICS IN RELATION TO:

Ratio of Mortgage Debt to Real Estate Assets, 108 Counties

(dollar figures in thousands)

	COUNTIES GROUPED BY RATIO OF MORTGAGE DEBT TO REAL ESTATE ASSETS			
	Counties			RATIO (%) OF HIGH 36 COUNTIES TO ALL COUNTIES
	High 36	Middle 36	Low 36	
Creditor interest in real estate assets	24%	18%	14%	126%
Economic Characteristics				
Physical assets per farm	$10.3	$7.4	$7.0	124%
Physical assets in:				
Land	51%	51%	55%	98%
Buildings	24	24	21	104
Non-real-estate	25	25	24	100
Cropland/total acreage[a]	49	42	29	122
Dwellings/farm real estate, 1930	16	18	15	100
Farm product value, 1939:				
Crops and livestock	66	60	63	105
Dairy products	16	13	10	123
Poultry and prod. and misc.	6	7	6	100
Used by farm household	12	19	21	67
Off-farm work in days, 1939[b]	27	36	43	77
Change in phys. asset value, 1930-1940[c]	−22%	−23%	−21%	100%
Financial Characteristics				
Interest in physical assets of:				
Operators	45%	49%	52%	94%
Landlords	29	28	29	100
Creditors	26	23	19	113
Mtgd. farms/all farms	51	43	34	119
Mtg. debt/value of mtgd. farms	44	41	35	110
Mtg. debt/value of all farms	24	18	14	126
Farm mtg. debt held by:				
FLB's and FFMC	45	51	44	96
Ins. and mtg. investment companies	16	10	9	133
Commercial and savings banks	8	12	10	80
Individuals and misc.	31	27	37	100
Non-real-estate loans, as % of total non-real-estate farm assets, of:				
Banks and PCA's	14	14	11	108
FSA and ECFL Division of FCA	6	10	8	75

(footnotes on next page)

Footnotes to Table 23

a Cropland excludes plowable pasture.

b Per farm operator.

c Data showing the ratio of mortgage debt to the value of all farm real estate and the change in value of physical farm assets, 1930-1940, based on a straight array of the counties, are shown below:

	High	Middle	Low
Mortgage debt/value of all farm real estate	25%	18%	13%
Change in value of physical assets, 1930-1940	−33	−17	−16

of the explanation for this high real estate debt doubtless can be found in the agricultural characteristics of the farms in these counties. What conditions permitted substantial real estate credit but discouraged landlord investment from compensating for the relatively low operator investment?

To find an answer to this question it is necessary to look for a combination of the following conditions: (1) capital requirements per farm high enough to require a substantial amount of outside capital, (2) circumstances tending either to discourage landlord investment or to require landlords to borrow extensively, and (3) an appropriate collateral basis for the extension of greater-than-average amounts of real estate credit.[6] The first condition is based on the assumption that in most counties with very small farms, only a moderate number of owners will need to borrow against their real estate, and the amount that they require, or will be able to obtain, will tend to be moderate in relation to the value of their real estate. The second two conditions might well be present among counties with a wide range of farm sizes. In most small-farm counties landlords would be reluctant to invest, whereas they would tend to borrow heavily in large-farm counties. As the third condition depends on lender standards, one might expect to find agriculture of widely different character meeting the collateral requirements of one or another type of lender on farm real estate. It would be unreasonable, therefore, to expect to find high real estate credit associated with any one particular economic characteristic of agriculture. Indeed one might expect to encounter real estate credit where several influences combine to work in that direction. These influences may be compounded out of many and diverse elements.

---

little difference between the "high" and "low" groups in the use of non-real-estate credit.

[6] The mortgage contract with an owner operator may shift enough of the risk of the farm business to the operator to permit capital to flow to types of agriculture that do not attract landlord investment.

Since summary tabulations like Table 23 fail to reveal clear-cut differences between the agriculture that makes extensive use of real estate credit and that which uses such credit relatively little, we have found it necessary to undertake a more detailed examination of the available data. A separate analysis of each of the three groups of 36 counties in Table 23 would be fraught with difficulties, as these have been especially arranged to reduce the influence on group comparisons of differential financial experience in the 1930's. For this reason our comparisons are confined to the "high" and "low" groups, in which contrasts are likely to be sufficiently sharp.

The following tabulation supports the hypothesis that relatively few of the small-farm counties are likely to have high real estate debt. The two small-farm counties shown in the high group—they are in Alabama—are near the bottom of an array of the high 36 counties.[7] The twelve counties with assets per farm less than $4,000 that fall in the low group are located in widely distributed areas—for example, northern Wisconsin and northern Minnesota; eastern Texas; low land-value counties in Arkansas, Mississippi, and Louisiana; southern Indiana and Kentucky; and Florida and Virginia.

ASSET SIZE OF FARM	NUMBER OF COUNTIES IN COUNTY GROUPS BY RATIO OF REAL ESTATE DEBT TO REAL ESTATE ASSETS	
	High 36	Low 36
Under $4,000	2	12
4,000 - 7,999	11	10
8,000 - 13,999	16	8
14,000 - 19,999	2	3
20,000 and over	5	3
Total	36	36

From an examination of the agriculture of these areas it is not difficult to fit most of these counties into a classification of agriculture which is not very attractive either as security for real estate loans or for outright investment by a nonoperator.

In the $4,000-to-$7,999 size-of-farm class the number in the high 36 counties differs very little from the number in the low 36. The following tabulation, however, which is based on the

[7] Their inclusion in the high group results from the regrouping of counties to equalize average asset change, 1930-1940, for the three groups of counties.

11 counties in this size group with high real estate debt and the 10 counties in the same size group with low real estate debt, suggests possible reasons for the difference.

	High 11 Counties	Low 10 Counties
Real estate debt/real estate assets	24%	14%
Change in value of farm assets, 1930-1940	—20	—29
Land value/total physical assets	41	55
Cropland/total acreage[a]	44	32
Farm product value, 1939:		
Crops and livestock	51	64
Dairy products	24	8

[a] Cropland excludes plowable pasture.

The explanation of the difference cannot be found in variations in financial experience in the 1930's, as the "low 10" counties had the more severe asset deflation. However, nonoperators would be less interested in owning the farms in the "high 11" counties than in acquiring property in the "low 10" counties. A higher proportion of the assets in the low counties was in the form of buildings and non-real-estate assets, and here also dairy farming was much more important. These same factors, particularly the necessity for larger investment in dairy herds and dairy equipment, might well give rise also to greater need for farm owner-operators to borrow on real estate security to finance these assets. Moreover, the larger cropland base in the "high 11" counties might well provide a more acceptable basis for real estate loans. The reasons for higher real estate debt in this case, therefore, may be found in differences in asset and product composition of the agriculture.

In the size group $8,000 to $13,999, which includes counties with larger average size than obtains in the sample as a whole, there were more counties in the "high real estate" group than in the "low" group. Furthermore, those in the "high" group had farms with average size of $10,800 compared with $9,090 in the "low" group. This finding supports the hypothesis that use of real estate credit is related to size of farm. Other comparisons are presented at the top of the next page.

Although dairy production is somewhat more important in the "high" than in the "low" group, the principal difference is in the greater proportion of acreage in cropland. Higher asset size in the high-credit-use group would work in the direction of greater need for outside funds, and a high cropland component of acreage would tend to provide the basis for more loans. The available data do not permit a separate evaluation of the relative strength of the "demand" and the "supply" influences suggested by these comparisons.

	High 16 Counties	Low 8 Counties
Real estate debt/real estate assets	23%	14%
Change in value of farm assets, 1930-1940	−25	−24
Land value/total physical assets	55	57
Cropland/total acreage[a]	54	27
Farm product value, 1939:		
Crops and livestock	70	69
Dairy products	14	12

[a] Cropland excludes plowable pasture.

Turning next to the two largest size groups, with assets per farm of $14,000 and over, we find seven counties in the high-real-estate-credit-use group and six counties in the low group, and average assets per farm somewhat larger in the high than in the low group—$23,000 as compared with about $20,000. Comparisons on other points are shown below:

	High 7 Counties	Low 6 Counties
Real estate debt/real estate assets	27%	15%
Change in value of farm assets, 1930-1940	−27	−19
Land value/total physical assets	57	64
Cropland/total acreage[a]	49	44
Farm product value, 1939:		
Crops and livestock	78	81
Dairy products	12	10

[a] Cropland excludes plowable pasture.

A part of the explanation of higher real estate debt in the seven-county group may be found in the larger asset size of farms and the greater farm asset deflation in the 1930's. A larger proportion of cropland also would improve the basis for real estate credit, whereas greater non-real-estate assets and somewhat more emphasis on dairying might further a greater use of real estate credit to finance non-real-estate assets. Although these comparative data indicate that the conditions set forth earlier for high real estate credit use are present in the seven-county group, the contrasts are not so sharp as in the case of the other size groups.

Another method of testing our multiple-factor hypothesis regarding the use of real estate credit is developed in the following tabulation, in which the nine counties that are "high" in respect to the ratio of real estate debt to total real estate assets have been selected from each asset-deflation quartile and their ratios compared with the average for the 27-county quartile as a whole.

ECONOMIC AND FINANCIAL CHARACTERISTICS	NINE COUNTIES WITH HIGHEST RATIOS OF REAL ESTATE DEBT TO TOTAL REAL ESTATE ASSETS[a] (AVERAGE FOR RESPECTIVE QUARTILE GROUP = 100)				
	Asset-Deflation Quartiles				AVERAGE OF QUARTILES
	1st	*2nd*	*3rd*	*4th*	
Real estate debt/total real estate assets	122	137	122	131	128
Physical assets per farm	131	120	123	132	127
Land as % of total assets	101	85	104	100	98
Cropland as % of total acreage[b]	127	131	98	140	124
Farm product value, 1939:					
Crops and livestock	105	92	107	115	105
Dairy products	101	164	109	94	117
Off-farm work in days, 1939[c]	72	74	97	64	77

[a] Data are for 1940 except where otherwise indicated.
[b] Cropland excludes plowable pasture.
[c] Per farm operator.

It appears from these comparisons that, even when counties are segregated according to their financial experience in the 1930's, larger-than-average farms are found in all four subclasses. This fact in itself warrants a presumption that a higher-than-average proportion of the funds invested in farm real estate would come from outside sources. But the reasons why these additional funds are supplied more heavily in the form of real estate credit, rather than landlord investment, must be sought in characteristics of the agriculture that tend to discourage investment by landlords but to encourage debt financing.

A factor that might help to explain the apparent reluctance of landlords to invest in farms in these nine counties may be that here the land component of total assets and the crop and livestock component of total product are relatively low in view of the larger-than-average size of the farms involved. Moreover, in three of the four county groups the proportion of cropland to total acreage is higher than average, thus providing a basis for greater use of real estate credit. Dairy product sales tend to

107

be more important in total product value than is the case with farms of average size, which might explain the heavier reliance on real estate as security for loans. Although the combination of characteristics is somewhat different in each quartile, the high level of real estate credit appears to be in conformity with the explanation offered earlier in this chapter.

As for low real estate debt in relation to the value of all real estate assets, this phenomenon cannot be consistently identified with a uniform pattern of farm economic characteristics, as we learn from the following tabulation. However, it is possible partially to explain a low percentage of real estate debt on the basis of limited need for outside capital or of conditions that would be more likely to encourage landlord investment, namely low average asset size and a relatively high proportion of assets in land in relation to size of farm. But since the third quartile does not exhibit the limiting factor of low cropland, it is necessary to seek out other characteristics of the agriculture that are not fully revealed by the data. For example, four of the nine counties fit reasonably well the concept of small-scale agriculture that would not be well suited to serve as security for large amounts of real estate credit; three others are located near large cities in the East where urban influences may have an effect; and two include agriculture that may be so attractive to landlord investment that little real estate credit is needed. Average ratios for small groups of counties do not show up these divergent limiting factors.

| | NINE COUNTIES WITH LOWEST RATIOS OF REAL ESTATE DEBT TO TOTAL REAL ESTATE ASSETS[a] (AVERAGE FOR RESPECTIVE QUARTILE GROUP = 100) | | | | |
| | Asset-Deflation Quartiles | | | | AVERAGE OF QUARTILES |
ECONOMIC AND FINANCIAL CHARACTERISTICS	1st	2nd	3rd	4th	
Real estate debt/total real estate assets	75	72	77	70	74
Physical assets per farm	71	95	101	67	84
Land as % of total assets	98	114	106	100	105
Cropland as % of total acreage[b]	65	64	96	67	73
Farm product value, 1939:					
Crops and livestock	97	112	97	91	99
Dairy products	93	55	82	99	82
Off-farm work in days, 1939[c]	124	133	92	145	124

[a] Data are for 1940 except where otherwise indicated.
[b] Cropland excludes plowable pasture.   [c] Per farm operator.

In order to illustrate further how a relatively high ratio of mortgage debt to value of real estate may result from different combinations of conditions that leave a gap in equity capital supply, we present in Table 24 a grouping of counties according to (1) the percentage of farms under mortgage, and (2) the ratio of mortgage debt to value of mortgaged farms. Each basis of classification results in groups of counties that differ substantially in respect to ratio of real estate debt to value of all farm real estate.

These two groupings illustrate a different combination of influences that appears to result in relatively high mortgage debt. The counties in which frequency of mortgage debt is highest tend to have large-scale farms, although the counties with larger-than-average assets per farm tend to differ little with respect to most of the indexes of asset and product composition. They are high, however, with respect to the cropland component of acreage. These observations appear to support the hypothesis that if relatively heavy capital requirements from outsiders are unaccompanied by conditions that will attract landlord investment, a gap in equity capital is left that will be filled by mortgage credit if the security is adequate.

Almost two thirds of the mortgage funds employed in these counties that have a high frequency of mortgage debt were supplied by centralized lenders—federal farm land banks, the Federal Farm Mortgage Corporation, and insurance companies —compared with about one half in the counties with a low frequency of such debt. Apparently, agriculture that tends to have high frequency of mortgage debt tends to attract more of its mortgage funds from a relatively broad capital market.

In the second case, where intensity of use of mortgage credit is the criterion, the two groups of counties do not differ much in average farm size; but asset and product characteristics seem to favor landlord investment less where the volume of mortgage debt is heavy in relation to real estate assets than where debt frequency is high. Although outside capital requirements appear to be smaller per farm than in the first case, mortgage credit demand remains strong as a result of a somewhat different set of conditions—a low land component of assets and a high non-crop and livestock component of farm product throw-off—that tend to discourage landlord investment. The relatively high cropland component of acreage in the high debt-to-value counties is favorable to extensive borrowing on real estate security. In-

TABLE 24

ECONOMIC AND FINANCIAL CHARACTERISTICS IN RELATION TO:

Percentage of Farms under Mortgage and Ratio of Mortgage Debt to Value of Mortgaged Farms
(*dollar figures in thousands*)

	COUNTIES GROUPED BY PER CENT OF FARMS UNDER MORTGAGE[a]		COUNTIES GROUPED BY RATIO (%) OF MORTGAGE DEBT TO VALUE OF MORT-GAGED FARMS[b]	
	High 36	*Low 36*	*High 36*	*Low 36*
Economic Characteristics				
Physical assets per farm	$11.1	$5.3	$8.9	$8.4
Physical assets in:				
Land	55%	52%	45%	60%
Buildings	22	22	27	19
Non-real-estate	23	26	28	21
Cropland/total acreage[c]	49	28	47	33
Dwellings/farm real estate, 1930	14	17	18	14
Farm product value, 1939:				
Crops and livestock	69	60	59	67
Dairy products	14	10	20	8
Poultry and prod. and misc.	6	6	7	6
Used by farm household	11	24	14	19
Off-farm work in days, 1939[d]	32	39	26	45
Change in phys. asset value, 1930-1940	—21%	—22%	—26%	—20%
Financial Characteristics				
Interest in physical assets of:				
Operators	45%	53%	47%	49%
Landlords	30	28	27	32
Creditors	25	19	26	19
Mtgd. farms/all farms	54	31	46	40
Mtg. debt/value of mtgd. farms	41	37	48	32
Mtg. debt/value of all farms	22	14	22	15
Farm mtg. debt held by:				
FLB's and FFMC	49	43	47	49
Ins. and mtg. investment companies	17	8	11	13
Commercial and savings banks	6	11	8	8
Individuals and miscellaneous	28	38	34	30
Non-real-estate loans, as % of total non-real-estate farm assets, of:				
Banks and PCA's	15	11	12	12
FSA and ECFL Division of FCA	7	9	9	7

(footnotes on next page)

Footnotes to Table 24

a Comparative data before regrouping of counties:

	High	Middle	Low
Mtgd. farm/total farms	54%	45%	31%
Change in physical asset value, 1930-1940	−26	−21	−19

b Comparative data before regrouping of counties.

	High	Middle	Low
Mtg. debt/value of mtgd. farms	50%	39%	31%
Change in phys. asset value, 1930-1940	−37	−20	−9

c Cropland excludes plowable pasture.

d Per farm operator.

surance companies provide a smaller percentage of the real estate loans, and banks and other local lenders a larger part, than in the counties in which debt frequency is highest.

Because average asset size of farm differs very little between the 36 counties with the highest, and the 36 with the lowest, ratios of mortgage debt to value of mortgaged farms, a further breakdown of these groups by size classes is presented below:

ASSET SIZE OF FARM	COUNTIES GROUPED BY RATIO OF MORTGAGE DEBT TO VALUE OF MORTGAGED FARMS	
	High 36	Low 36
Under $4,000	3	10
4,000 - 7,999	16	9
8,000 - 13,999	13	8
14,000 - 19,999	1	4
20,000 and over	3	5
Total	36	36

Whereas 29 of the counties in the "high" group fall within the range of $4,000 to $13,999, only 17 in the low group come within this range. The average asset size in the "low 36" group reflects the offsetting influence of 10 counties with asset size of farms less than $4,000 and 9 counties with asset size of $14,000 and over. Most of the 10 small-farm counties are in the poorer land areas of the South. The 9 large-farm counties are predominantly range livestock counties and cash grain counties. Some of the former may not provide adequate security for a large volume of conventional real estate credit, whereas others of the latter type would appear to be so attractive to landlord investment that less-than-average amounts of real estate credit would be used.

111

Differences with respect to importance of credit sources between the "high 36" counties in each of the two classifications in Table 24 suggests that real estate credit may still be too broad a category for the most fruitful analysis of credit use by agriculture. In both groups real estate debt amounts to 22 per cent of all real estate assets, but where the criterion is high debt-frequency, more of the debt is held by centralized lenders such as insurance companies and land banks than when the criterion is high debt-to-value ratios. Differences in sources of credit suggest that the function performed by real estate credit in the one case may be different from that in the other. It seems probable that more of the credit in the "high 36" counties grouped by debt frequency performs the function of financing real estate ownership than in the "high 36" counties based on debt-to-value ratios. In the latter counties the use of funds probably is less closely related to the security on which credit is obtained. This difference in the nature of the real estate credit may explain in part the fact that extensive use of such credit is found in rather divergent types of agriculture.

While the foregoing examination of the 108 counties identifies a number of factors which appear to influence the extent to which real estate credit is used to finance agriculture, the available evidence does not indicate the relative strength of these several influences. It does, however, suggest strongly that the extent to which agriculture is financed with real estate credit is related systematically to its economic characteristics and the reactions of capital users and suppliers to these characteristics.

More adequate data would doubtless enable us to identify still other relationships between real estate credit and type of agriculture. For example, it has not been possible to take account of the relationship of variability of crop yields to use of real estate credit, because no satisfactory basis could be found for a comparison of different kinds of agriculture. Since the method employed to make county groups comparable with respect to financial experience in the 1930's may not take full account of differences among the Great Plains counties in yield variability, any separate influence of this factor on use of real estate credit becomes obscured in group comparisons. However, limited evidence obtained by enlarging the sample of wheat counties in a separate study did not indicate any marked difference in use of real estate credit between county groups classified on the basis of extent of crop abandonment.[8] It is likely that yield variability may have more influence on the source from which real estate credit is drawn than on the total use of such credit in relation to real estate assets.

Despite the shortcomings of the present analysis, it is believed that it points to the direction in which a more complete explanation of variations in real estate credit use may be found. The major part of the capital that is applied to the financing of farm real estate comes from owner operators and landlords. High real estate debt, moreover, cannot be explained solely by the attitudes of lender groups toward particular kinds of agriculture. In fact, the evidence presented here suggests that agriculture that would appear to be most attractive as security for real estate loans may draw upon only moderate amounts of such credit. On the other hand, heavy real estate debt often occurs in agriculture that does not measure up to the highest standards of security for real estate loans, perhaps reflecting reluctance of equity investors to extend financing. A full explanation of variations in the use of real estate credit, therefore, must take into account the important part that demand for this form of credit plays in determining the extent of its use.

Non-Real-Estate Loans in Relation to Non-Real-Estate Assets

Certain deficiencies in the data make it more difficult to establish differences in the use of non-real-estate credit than in the use of mortgage credit. With regard to the former, data are available only for the four major lending agencies. Moreover, since this is predominantly short-term and seasonal credit, data taken at a given point in time do not necessarily reveal the average amount of credit in use over an extended period. A further difficulty arises with respect to the data for commercial and savings banks, which are tabulated on the basis of the location of the bank making the loan rather than the location of the farm on which the loan is extended. Thus some county data may include loans made on farms in adjoining counties. In view of the foregoing considerations, small differences that may be noted between county groups are unlikely to be of much significance.

It is impossible to determine on the basis of present information how accurately variations among counties in the importance of

[8] Donald C. Horton, "Adaptation of the Farm Capital Structure to Uncertainty," *Journal of Farm Economics*, February 1949, pp. 76-100.

non-real-estate loans of the four agencies reflect variations in total use of non-real-estate credit.[9] It appears unlikely that variations among counties in the importance of bank and PCA loans alone would be revelatory in this respect, as both types of lenders are limited in their ability to extend credit to many of the farmers who tend to rely heavily on credit from local merchants and other nonfinancial lenders. Inclusion of the loans of the two special purpose lenders tends to take account of credit use in some areas that would not be reflected in the bank and PCA loans, but it also introduces other complications. By 1940, Farm Security Administration or emergency crop-and-feed loans had accumulated to such high levels in some counties that the amounts held by these lenders overemphasized the extent of total credit use. This latter difficulty is partially overcome when county groups are balanced to include about the same frequency distribution of counties by financial experience in the 1930's, but this adjustment probably is far from a perfect correction for the accumulation of past-due loans by these emergency credit agencies. Despite these heavy handicaps, it is believed that the data on non-real-estate loans of the four lender groups have value for the present analysis.

[9] Because the volume of non-real-estate loans held by lenders other than the four for which data are shown could be estimated only on an approximate basis which involved considerable judgment, it was decided not to base the analysis on estimated total non-real-estate debt. However, these separate estimates may have some analytical value. The percentage ratios below, computed from a classification of counties in which the high and the low 36 are selected on the basis of the percentage of total physical assets represented by non-real-estate farm assets, throw some light on the extent to which the ratio of non-real-estate debt to total debt varies with the importance of non-real-estate assets in total assets.

	High 36	Low 36
Non-real-estate assets/total physical assets	32%	18%
Real estate assets/total physical assets	68	82
Non-real-estate debt/total debt	44	30
Real estate debt/total debt	56	70
Non-real-estate debt/non-real-estate assets	32	36
Real estate debt/real estate assets	19	18

These computations suggest that the proportions of total debt represented by real estate and non-real-estate debt vary with the proportion of total assets in the two categories. But the ratio of non-real-estate debt to non-real-estate assets is lower when non-real-estate assets are a relatively high, than when they are a relatively low, proportion of total assets. It is probable that real estate debt is used to finance non-real-estate assets to a greater extent when such assets constitute a high proportion of the total.

Some light is thrown on the question of the kinds of agriculture in which non-real-estate farm loans tend to be high in relation to total non-real-estate farm assets by the tabulation on page 116, which uses alternative bases for classification of the 108 counties.

From this summary it is found that the combined credit ratio for the four agencies is relatively high under the following conditions: (1) low average assets per farm, (2) a high land component of assets, (3) a high crop and livestock component of total product, (4) a low dairy product component of total product, (5) low off-farm work per farm operator, and (6) low operator and high landlord interest in physical assets. Little difference is observed as between the high 36 and the low 36 when the 108 counties are grouped according to cropland component of acreage and home consumption of farm products. Nor are the differences very marked when the non-real-estate component of assets or the real estate credit ratios are employed as bases of classification.

It will be noted that whereas earlier tabulations indicate that high average size of farm and high land component of physical assets tend to go together, in the summary breakdown the high average size group shows the lower non-real-estate credit ratio and the high land component of assets the higher ratio. It will be noted also that the level of the non-real-estate credit ratio tends to be associated with differences in the relative importance of operator and landlord interests in physical assets. These relationships suggest that a further subclassification of certain of the major three-group tabulations might bring out more fully patterns of association between economic characteristics of agriculture and the non-real-estate credit ratio.

When the 36 large-size farm counties are divided into those with a "high" and those with a "low" land component of assets, it is apparent that non-real-estate credit is used more heavily in the former (Table 25). This can be explained, perhaps, in terms of certain economic characteristics of the agriculture that tend to attract investment by landlords and by insurance and mortgage companies. Since landlord ownership is more prevalent in these "high" counties, it is to be expected that the loans to the operator should be secured more frequently by non-real-estate assets or made on an unsecured basis. On the other hand large-farm counties, in which the land component of assets is low, have asset and product characteristics usually associated with high operator investment. There is reason to believe that in these counties real

115

BASIS FOR CLASSIFICATION OF 108 COUNTIES INTO THREE HIGH, MIDDLE, AND LOW COUNTY GROUPS	NON-REAL-ESTATE FARM LOANS, AS % OF TOTAL NON-REAL-ESTATE FARM ASSETS		
	Banks & PCA's	FSA and ECFL Office of FCA	Total, Four Lenders
Physical assets per farm			
High 36	14	4	18
Low 36	13	12	25
Land value/total physical assets			
High 36	16	7	23
Low 36	10	6	16
Cropland/total acreage[a]			
High 36	13	7	20
Low 36	13	7	20
Non-real-estate assets/total physical assets[a]			
High 36	9	9	18
Low 36	16	5	21
Sales of crops and livestock/value of product			
High 36	17	6	23
Low 36	9	6	15
Sales of dairy products/value of product			
High 36	9	6	15
Low 36	15	8	23
Home consumption/value of product			
High 36	12	9	21
Low 36	15	6	21
Off-farm work per operator			
High 36	11	5	16
Low 36	15	7	22
Operators interest in physical assets			
High 36	9	4	13
Low 36	18	11	29
Landlord interest in physical assets[a]			
High 36	16	7	23
Low 36	10	5	15
Mortgaged farms/all farms			
High 36	15	7	22
Low 36	11	9	20
Mortgage debt/value of mortgaged farms			
High 36	12	9	21
Low 36	12	7	19
Mortgage debt/value of all real estate			
High 36	14	6	20
Low 36	11	7	18

[a] Not shown separately elsewhere.

TABLE 25

ECONOMIC AND FINANCIAL CHARACTERISTICS IN RELATION TO:

Farm Asset Size, and Percentage of Assets in Land, 108 Counties

(dollar figures in thousands)

	HIGH 36 COUNTIES BY ASSET SIZE GROUPED BY % OF ASSETS IN LAND		MIDDLE 36 COUNTIES BY ASSET SIZE GROUPED BY % OF ASSETS IN LAND		LOW 36 COUNTIES BY ASSET SIZE GROUPED BY % OF ASSETS IN LAND	
	High 18	Low 18	High 18	Low 18	High 18	Low 18
Economic Characteristics						
Physical assets per farm	$17.5	$14.2	$7.3	$7.3	$4.0	$4.2
Physical assets in:						
Land	68%	47%	61%	38%	57%	42%
Buildings	13	24	17	35	20	29
Non-real-estate	19	29	22	27	23	29
Cropland/total acreage[a]	48	42	37	46	34	32
Dwellings/farm real estate, 1930	9	14	12	23	16	23
Farm product value, 1939:						
Crops and livestock	84	66	70	51	61	47
Dairy products	5	19	7	23	6	19
Poultry and prod. and misc.	3	5	6	11	5	7
Used by farm household	8	10	17	15	28	27
Off-farm work in days, 1939[b]	29	30	34	42	34	43
Change in phys. asset value, 1930-1940	—18%	—23%	—27%	—20%	—20%	—24%

(concluded on next page)

TABLE 25 (concluded)

	HIGH 36 COUNTIES BY ASSET SIZE GROUPED BY % OF ASSETS IN LAND		MIDDLE 36 COUNTIES BY ASSET SIZE GROUPED BY % OF ASSETS IN LAND		LOW 36 COUNTIES BY ASSET SIZE GROUPED BY % OF ASSETS IN LAND	
	High 18	Low 18	High 18	Low 18	High 18	Low 18
Financial Characteristics						
Interest in physical assets of:						
Operators	37%	50%	42%	58%	45%	59%
Landlords	40	27	33	22	32	18
Creditors	23	23	25	20	23	23
Mtgd. farms/all farms	51	45	44	43	35	39
Mtg. debt/value of mtgd. farms	35	42	42	43	37	40
Mtg. debt/value of all farms	20	21	19	19	16	16
Farm mtg. debt held by:						
FLB's and FFMC	51	40	50	39	54	49
Ins. and mtg. investment companies	24	12	15	7	8	4
Commercial and savings banks	5	10	6	15	12	12
Individuals and miscellaneous	20	38	29	39	26	35
Non-real-estate loans, as % of total non-real-estate farm assets, of:						
Banks and PCA's	18	11	16	9	14	11
FSA and ECFL Division of FCA	5	3	11	4	12	12

a Cropland excludes plowable pasture.
b Per farm operator.

estate is used more frequently as collateral for loans to provide short- and intermediate-term funds for operating purposes.[10]

Much the same pattern of relationships between the economic characteristics of farming and the use of non-real-estate credit is found among the middle-sized farm counties; but among the small-farm counties differences in the use of non-real-estate credit are less evident as between counties that are "high" and "low" in land component of assets. This latter finding may be attributable to the smaller margin of difference in the land component of assets in these counties, or to the contrast in their previous financial experience; there was, for example, a large volume of FSA and ECF loans in the low land component groups. It seems probable, however, that small-farm counties exhibit less differentiation between the use of mortgage and non-real-estate credit than do large-farm counties.[11]

In the foregoing analysis we have treated real estate and non-real-estate credit as if each were a homogeneous type of financing. In the next chapter the two forms of credit are broken down according to the character of the lending agency, so that we may try to determine whether there is any evidence that lenders tend to specialize among different types of agriculture.

[10] As can be seen from Table 25, much the same patterns of relationships would be found if the three sets of counties grouped according to asset size of farms had been subclassified according to the importance of crop and livestock sales in total value of product. Similarly, the interest of either operators or landlords in total assets could be used. The land component of total assets is employed because it brings into view contrasting characteristics of agriculture which appear to be associated with differences in the use of non-real-estate credit.

[11] Relationships of non-real-estate credit to nature of the agriculture are considered further in Chapter 6 in connection with an analysis by major lender groups.

CREDIT SOURCES IN RELATION TO ECONOMIC CHARACTERISTICS OF THE AGRICULTURE

THE principal farm lending agencies differ significantly in organization, in the character of the funds they invest, and in basic objectives. It is not surprising, therefore, that they should differ also with respect to the kinds of agriculture they finance. One would not expect commercial banks, for instance, to lend heavily on the types of farm real estate toward which insurance companies direct the greater part of their mortgage lending; nor would one expect private credit institutions to operate in the field served primarily by federal or federally sponsored agencies.

The object of the present chapter is to present the available evidence concerning functional specialization among lenders in the farm capital market. It must be recognized, however, that the distribution of total loans by different lender groups in 1940 was influenced by the experience of the 1930's, and that similar information for a later date might show a somewhat different pattern of specialization, particularly with regard to governmental credit agencies.

Mortgage Lending Agencies

The percentage of farm mortgage loans held by particular lender groups varies from one set of counties to another, indicating that there is some degree of functional specialization among lenders. The character of this specialization is revealed in Tables 26 and 27, which have been assembled from data presented earlier.

It is evident at once that banks and insurance companies tend to play complementary roles. Banks appear to hold a higher-than-average proportion of total outstanding mortgage loans in counties where (1) farms are of moderate size, (2) land is of less-than-average importance as a component of total assets, (3) dairy and miscellaneous products are of more-, and crops and livestock are of less-, than-average importance in total farm output, and (4) farm-home consumption of farm products and off-farm work are relatively high. Insurance companies, on the other hand, tend to hold high percentages of total outstanding loans where (1) farms are large, (2) a high proportion of farm assets is in land, and cropland constitutes a relatively large proportion of total acreage, (3) crop and livestock sales are greater than average in relation to sales of dairy and miscellaneous products, and (4) both home consumption of farm products and incidence of off-farm work are low.

As regards the financial characteristics of counties in which banks and insurance companies tend to specialize, the highest percentages of outstanding farm mortgage loans appear to be held by banks in counties where operator interest is high and landlord interest is low. But banks hold a relatively low percentage of the total loans where the per cent of farms under mortgage is high. As for the insurance companies, they hold large percentages of all outstanding loans where landlord investment is high and operator interest is low, and where the percentage of mortgaged farms is high. No evidence of specialization by either lender group is found in areas of high or low debt-to-value ratios for mortgaged farms.

The tendency of banks and insurance companies to concentrate their mortgage lending according to certain economic characteristics of the agriculture served is often presented as regional specialization. Thus, banks lend more in the Northeast and insurance companies in the Corn Belt. An examination of the data for separate regions indicates similar patterns of specialization also within broad regions. For example, when the 26 counties of the sample that are located in the East South Central and South Atlantic states are classified according to the importance of land as a component of assets, the following results are obtained:

LAND AS A PER CENT OF TOTAL ASSETS	NUMBER OF COUNTIES	PER CENT OF FARM MORTGAGE DEBT HELD BY:	
		Insurance Companies	*Banks*
55 - 69%	8	21%	9%
48 - 54	10	7	17
35 - 47	8	4	25

In other regions, however, the ratio of land to total assets does not classify counties into groups with the same pattern of lender specialization as that shown for the entire 108 counties. For example, the ratio of cropland to total acreage classifies county groups in the West South Central states by importance of insurance company loans whereas the land-to-asset ratio does not. This

TABLE 26

Percentage of Total Farm Mortgage Debt in 1940 Held by Designated Lender Groups, 108 Counties Classified into High, Middle, and Low Thirds According to Selected Economic Characteristics

PERCENTAGE OF FARM MORTGAGE DEBT HELD BY:[a]

BASIS FOR CLASSIFICATION INTO COUNTY GROUPS	Commercial and Savings Banks in:			Individuals and Miscellaneous in:			FLB's and FFMC in:			Insurance and Mtg. Investment Companies in:		
	High 36	Middle 36	Low 36	High 36	Middle 36	Low 36	High 36	Middle 36	Low 36	High 36	Middle 36	Low 36
Physical assets per farm	7%	10%	12%	29%	34%	31%	45%	45%	51%	19%	11%	6%
Land/physical assets[b]	5	11	13	24	31	38	50	47	43	21	11	6
Cropland/total acreage[c]	8	12	9	26	31	37	46	46	48	20	11	6
Farm product value, 1939:												
Crops and livestock	6	9	14	27	26	40	48	55	38	19	10	8
Dairy products	12	9	7	37	30	25	44	50	48	7	11	20
Used by farm household	12	10	7	31	34	29	48	44	47	9	12	17
Off-farm work in days, 1939[d]	12	11	7	38	29	27	43	50	46	7	10	20

a In order to prevent differential financial experience in the 1930's from affecting the analysis, high, middle, and low groups of counties each contain about the same distribution of counties according to previous financial experience.
b Excluding buildings.
c Cropland excludes plowable pasture.
d Per farm operator.

TABLE 27

Percentage of Total Farm Mortgage Debt in 1940 Held by Designated Lender Groups, 108 Counties Classified into High, Middle, and Low Thirds According to Selected Financial Characteristics

PERCENTAGE OF FARM MORTGAGE DEBT HELD BY:[a]

BASIS FOR CLASSIFICATION INTO COUNTY GROUPS	Commercial and Savings Banks in:			Individuals and Miscellaneous in:			FLB's and FFMC in:			Insurance and Mtg. Investment Companies in:		
	High 36	Middle 36	Low 36	High 36	Middle 36	Low 36	High 36	Middle 36	Low 36	High 36	Middle 36	Low 36
Interest in physical assets of:												
Operators	12%	11%	6%	37%	32%	25%	43%	44%	52%	8%	13%	17%
Landlords	6	10	14	28	27	38	46	53	41	20	10	7
Creditors	8	11	10	28	32	34	54	41	44	10	16	12
Creditor interest/total outside interests[b]	11	9	9	36	27	30	48	47	43	5	17	18
Real estate debt/total outside interests in real estate	9	11	8	36	26	31	45	51	45	10	12	16
Per cent of farms mtgd.	6	12	11	28	28	38	49	47	43	17	13	8
Mtg. debt/value of mtgd. farms	8	12	8	34	29	30	47	44	49	11	15	13
Mtg. debt/value of all farms	8	12	10	31	27	37	45	51	44	16	10	9

[a] In order to prevent differential financial experience in the 1930's from affecting the analysis, high, middle, and low groups of counties each contain about the same distribution of counties according to previous financial experience.

[b] Outside interests are the combined interests of creditors and nonoperating owners.

123

is explained mainly by the fact that the county group with the highest land-to-asset ratios includes a number of Texas range livestock and high-risk wheat counties in which insurance companies lend very little. The land-to-asset ratio, however, distinguishes clearly between county groups in this region according to importance of bank mortgage loans.

The federal and federally sponsored lending agencies show less tendency to specialization of the foregoing type than do banks and insurance companies, but a few points may be noted. Like banks, these agencies tend to be relatively more important as lenders in counties with farms of smaller-than-average size. But with respect to the importance of land in total assets, crop and livestock sales, and off-farm work, their behavior resembles that of the insurance companies. Like the insurance companies, also, these lenders held a higher proportion of the farm mortgage debt in counties in which operator interest in assets was low in 1940; and again like the insurance companies, they held relatively more mortgage loans in counties where the frequency of mortgage debt was highest. But because these lenders' mortgage holdings in 1940 reflect the refinancing operations of the 1930's, such evidence of specialization by type of agriculture and financial characteristics of farms may not apply to other periods.

Individual and miscellaneous lenders likewise appear to specialize less than banks and insurance companies, although such specialization as is found appears to be more like that of banks than that of insurance companies. However, if the data could be broken down to show separately loans by local and absentee individuals, the former would probably be found to invest most extensively in counties like those in which banks take the lead, while the latter would probably tend to specialize in counties with agricultural patterns similar to those which attract insurance company investment.

Unlike the three other classes of lenders, individuals and miscellaneous lenders appear to invest most heavily in areas where the cropland component is low. When the counties are grouped into thirds according to the ratio of cropland to total acreage, it is found that this lender group holds the highest percentage of total mortgages in the 36 counties in which the cropland ratio is low, whereas banks hold the highest percentage in the middle third of the counties in this array. An examination of the low-cropland counties reveals that most of them possess characteristics of agriculture that might discourage bank lending on real estate.

Included in these are the range livestock counties, most of those in the poorer land areas of the East and South, a number of high-risk wheat counties, and others in which bank failures in the 1920's and 1930's were numerous. Although the evidence is not clear in all cases, it appears that individual lenders provide mortgage credit in a number of situations where banks are unwilling or unsuited to supply the kind of loan sought.

Because specialization of lenders in 1940 was related also to financial experience in the 1930's, selected comparisons are presented in Table 28 by major asset-deflation classes. From the 27 counties with greatest asset deflation in the 1930's (first quartile), the nine that were highest in percentage of mortgage debt held by banks are first selected and any distinctive economic characteristics of these nine counties are then indicated by relatives based on the entire 27 counties as 100.

Within the first quartile (greatest assets deflation), the nine counties in which banks stand out as sources of mortgage credit differ most sharply from those in which insurance companies stand out with respect to the importance of sales of dairy products. The bank counties had larger average asset-size farms than the insurance company counties in this quartile, though the difference between them in respect of crop and livestock sales is small. That the land bank and Federal Farm Mortgage Corporation counties ranked higher than the insurance company counties with respect to asset size, importance of land in total assets, and importance of cropland and of crop and livestock sales probably reflects the shifting of insurance company mortgages to the federal agencies in the 1930's.[1]

Turning next to the 27-county group that experienced the least asset deflation in the 1930's, we note that the counties in which banks were most important as lenders differed from those in which insurance companies predominated more in respect of size of farm than in importance of dairy products. In this grouping, sale of dairy products is more effective in identifying the counties in which individuals and miscellaneous lenders are outstanding.

As can be seen from the average of the relatives for the four quartiles, there appears to be a tendency for individuals and

[1] It probably reflects also the fact that insurance companies have never been important sources of mortgage credit in some of the counties with large livestock farms and in other large-crop farm counties characterized by high production risks growing out of wide variations in rainfall.

TABLE 28

Nine Counties with Highest Ratios of Mortgage Debt of a Specified Type of Lender to Total Real Estate Debt Compared with Quartile Groups of Counties Ranked by Asset Deflation

| | NINE COUNTIES WITH HIGHEST RATIOS OF MORTGAGE LOANS OF SPECIFIED TYPE OF LENDER TO TOTAL REAL ESTATE DEBT (AVG. FOR RESPECTIVE QUARTILE GROUP = 100) | | | | |
| | Asset-Deflation Quartiles[a] | | | | Average of Quartiles |
ECONOMIC CHARACTERISTICS AND LENDER GROUP	1st	2nd	3rd	4th	
Physical assets per farm					
Commercial and savings banks	118	69	108	47	85
Individuals and miscellaneous	75	126	81	101	95
FLB's and FFMC	113	89	72	117	97
Ins. and mtg. investment companies	98	120	108	115	110
Land in % of total physical assets					
Commercial and savings banks	90	94	83	89	89
Individuals and miscellaneous	88	92	85	104	92
FLB's and FFMC	110	120	119	100	110
Ins. and mtg. investment companies	105	112	120	108	111
Cropland in % of total acreage					
Commercial and savings banks	99	104	97	71	93
Individuals and miscellaneous	66	74	92	79	78
FLB's and FFMC	127	83	87	149	111
Ins. and mtg. investment companies	121	130	122	135	127
Sales of crops and livestock in % of total value of product					
Commercial and savings banks	90	91	89	87	89
Individuals and miscellaneous	89	97	69	101	89
FLB's and FFMC	116	112	119	100	112
Ins. and mtg. investment companies	96	109	122	111	109
Sales of dairy products in % of total value of product					
Commercial and savings banks	160	116	130	82	122
Individuals and miscellaneous	123	140	166	131	140
FLB's and FFMC	74	48	42	110	69
Ins. and mtg. investment companies	83	71	51	64	57

[a] The 108 counties were arrayed by degree of asset deflation in the 1930's, from greatest to least, and divided into quartiles. For each quartile the nine counties that were highest with respect to the ratios of mortgage loans of the specified type of lender to total real estate debt are compared with the average for the quartile group as a whole in this respect.

126

miscellaneous lenders to specialize in somewhat the same kinds of agriculture as those in which banks specialize. Federal land banks and the Federal Farm Mortgage Corporation, on the other hand, tended to concentrate their loans in the kinds of agriculture in which insurance companies lend most heavily. These averages, however, should be interpreted in the light of the fact that considerable variation is found among the quartiles in the relation of agricultural characteristics to particular lender groups. For example, on an average basis, banks appear to have held relatively more mortgages in the smaller-farm counties (as shown also in Table 26), but by quartiles the average size of farms in the bank counties ranged from 47 to 118 per cent of that for all counties in the quartile. This supplemental tabulation indicates that broad generalizations with respect to specialization of lenders by size of farm are likely to be subject to more qualifications when applied to regions than are generalizations with respect to specialization by other economic characteristics of agriculture.

The quartile comparisons in Table 28 also suggest the probability that functional specialization tends to be most evident when certain combinations of farm characteristics are made the basis of comparison. This is illustrated by the kinds of agriculture in the second and third quartiles in which individuals and miscellaneous lenders rank highest as sources of mortgage loans. In the second quartile the counties in which these lenders rank highest include a combination of large range livestock and large dairy farms, whereas in the third quartile the farms are smaller than average but dairy products are a relatively more important source of income. It is to be expected that this residual lender group would rank high as a source of mortgage loans in a wide range of situations where, for a variety of reasons, farm real estate is not well adapted to serve as security for loans by either local or centralized lending institutions.

Regional factors that are associated mainly with nonagricultural factors, such as greater availability of local funds for investment in farm mortgages in the older and more industrialized areas, doubtless exert some influence on the pattern of specialization in farm lending. Then there are differences among kinds of farming with respect to production and price risks; these factors have an important bearing on financing, though they could not be brought directly into the analysis by means of specific indicators.[2]

[2] For an attempt to evaluate these factors, see Donald C. Horton, "Adaptation of the Farm Capital Structure to Uncertainty," *Journal of Farm Economics*, February 1949, pp. 76-100.

Ratio of Lender Groups' Mortgage Holdings
to Value of Real Estate

We may carry the analysis of specialization still further by dividing our sample of 108 counties into groups of 36 according to which of the four types of lender had the highest ratio of mortgage loans to total value of real estate, and by comparing the characteristics of the agriculture among the counties so grouped. In some respects comparisons based on classifications in which lenders' mortgage holdings are related to total value of real estate are more meaningful than those based on percentages of total mortgage debt held by different lender groups. On the latter basis, for example, a county would be placed in the "high" group whenever loans by a particular type of lender constituted a large part of the total debt, even though this debt might be relatively small in relation to total real estate assets. Classified on the former basis, the "high" group comprises only those counties in which the particular lender is a relatively important source of total capital invested in farm real estate. The data for such a comparison of mortgage holdings are given in Table 29.

The chances are fairly good that observable differences in farm asset and product characteristics between counties in which mortgage loans of banks and insurance companies rank high signify real functional specialization in farm mortgage lending; but the average of asset and product percentages in counties shown for the other two lender groups fall so close to those for the entire sample that the evidence of specialization is less clear-cut.

As compared with the counties in which farm real estate loans held by insurance and mortgage investment companies are highest in relation to real estate assets, those counties in which bank loan percentages are highest give evidence of having farms whose buildings and non-real-estate assets are relatively important, whose receipts from dairy product sales are higher, comparatively, and in which the number of days of off-farm work is also relatively high.

The fact that the 36 counties in which federal agency loan ratios are highest exhibit characteristics of agriculture that fall near the average for the 108-county sample appears to reflect the multiple functions of these lending institutions. It should be noted also that conditions prevailing in the 1930's brought them mortgages on all types of farm businesses. A higher-than-average

TABLE 29

ECONOMIC AND FINANCIAL CHARACTERISTICS:

Four Groups of 36 Counties in Which Real Estate Loans of a Specified Type of Lender Were Highest in Relation to Total Real Estate Assets

(dollar figures in thousands)

	Commercial & Savings Banks	Individuals and Miscellaneous	FLB's and FFMC	Insurance & Mtg. Investment Companies
Real estate loans of lenders as % of:				
Total real estate assets[a]	3.4%	9.6%	13.1%	5.6%
Total real estate loans	19	46	61	27
Economic Characteristics				
Physical assets per farm	$8.7	$8.0	$8.5	$10.3
Physical assets in:				
Land	44%	48%	53%	59%
Buildings	29	26	22	20
Non-real-estate	27	26	25	21
Cropland /total acreage[b]	40	37	45	51
Dwellings/farm real estate, 1930	21	17	15	13
Farm product value, 1939:				
Crops and livestock	54	58	67	72
Dairy products	20	21	12	8
Poultry and prod. and misc.	7	7	4	6
Used by farm household	19	14	17	14
Off-farm work in days, 1939[c]	40	39	30	28
Change in phys. asset value, 1930-1940[d]	−21%	−22%	−23%	−22%
Financial Characteristics				
Interest in physical assets of:				
Operators	54%	52%	43%	42%
Landlords	24	27	30	35
Creditors	22	21	26	23
Mtgd. farms/all farms	42	44	47	48
Mtg. debt/value of mtgd. farms	41	41	43	40
Mtg. debt/value of all farms	19	21	22	21
Non-real-estate loans, as % of total non-real-estate farm assets, of:				
Banks and PCA's	14	11	14	15
FSA and ECFL Division of FCA	6	4	11	5

(footnotes on next page)

129

Footnotes to Table 29

a Counties were selected so that each group had, on the average, about the same degree of asset deflation in the 1930's.

b Cropland excludes plowable pasture.

c Per farm operator.

d Comparable data on the ratio of real estate loans of designated lenders to total real estate assets, based on a straight array of the counties, are shown below:

	Commercial & Savings Banks	Individuals and Miscellaneous	FLB's and FFMC	Insurance & Mtg. Investment Companies
Change in physical asset value, 1930-1940	−19%	−26%	−30%	−21%
Real estate loans/real estate assets	3.4	9.7	13.8	5.8

percentage of refinanced mortgages came from areas in the Middle West where farms had previously drawn heavily on insurance company loans, and when these were added to the loans the agencies already held—which had been made with the primary objective of providing credit in areas not usually served by the private institutional lenders—the result was a general coverage of all types of farms.

Finally, we note that counties whose ratios of individual and miscellaneous lenders' loans to total real estate assets are highest tend to show percentages approximating averages for the entire sample. This tendency is probably best explained by the diversity of investors included in this general category.

Table 30, which is constructed in the same manner as Table 28, permits further analysis of functional specialization among counties within the four asset-deflation classes. Here we find, for example, that when a high ratio of loans held by a specific lender group is made the basis for the selection of nine-county groups, farms in the bank counties are consistently smaller in asset size than those in the insurance company counties. Apparently, to combine the high nine counties of each 27-county quartile into a single 36-county group as we did in Table 29 does not seriously distort the comparisons.[3]

As the first and second quartiles are weighted heavily with counties in the central portion of the country, some of the differences between the kinds of agriculture in which banks and in-

[3] Averaging the relatives rather than the absolute data produces some differences in relationships as a result of different weighting, but the general pattern remains the same. This is seen most clearly in the case of the relatives for asset size of farm for the bank group.

TABLE 30

ECONOMIC CHARACTERISTICS:

Nine Counties with Highest Ratio of Mortgage Loans of a Specified Type of Lender to Total Real Estate Assets Compared with Quartile Groups of Counties Ranked by Asset Deflation

ECONOMIC CHARACTERISTICS AND LENDER GROUP	NINE COUNTIES WITH HIGHEST RATIOS OF MORTGAGE LOANS OF SPECIFIED TYPE OF LENDER TO TOTAL REAL ESTATE ASSETS (AVG. FOR RESPECTIVE QUARTILE GROUP = 100)				
	Asset-Deflation Quartiles[a]				Average of Quartiles
	1st	2nd	3rd	4th	
Physical assets per farm					
Commercial and savings banks	112	99	107	47	92
Individuals and miscellaneous	101	117	88	120	106
FLB's and FFMC	115	121	72	93	100
Ins. and mtg. investment companies	124	120	117	144	126
Land in % of total physical assets					
Commercial and savings banks	93	84	73	88	85
Individuals and miscellaneous	92	86	76	110	91
FLB's and FFMC	109	94	118	88	102
Ins. and mtg. investment companies	107	114	121	112	113
Cropland in % of total acreage					
Commercial and savings banks	115	123	91	71	100
Individuals and miscellaneous	78	101	94	94	92
FLB's and FFMC	126	124	86	113	112
Ins. and mtg. investment companies	115	130	120	146	128
Sales of crops and livestock in % of total value of product					
Commercial and savings banks	89	84	81	87	85
Individuals and miscellaneous	104	88	70	109	93
FLB's and FFMC	126	124	86	113	112
Ins. and mtg. investment companies	104	107	126	120	114
Sales of dairy products in % of total value of product					
Commercial and savings banks	157	160	157	82	139
Individuals and miscellaneous	129	169	185	101	146
FLB's and FFMC	83	127	46	146	100
Ins. and mtg. investment companies	78	67	50	42	59

[a] The 108 counties were arrayed by degree of asset deflation in the 1930's, from greatest to least, and divided into quartiles. For each quartile the nine counties with the highest ratio of mortgage loans of specified type of lender to total real estate assets are compared with the average for the quartile group as a whole in this respect.

131

surance company loans are high in relation to real estate value have a different meaning than those found in the third and fourth quartiles, which are more heavily weighted with southern and eastern states. For example, in the first and second quartiles the cropland ratio is higher than average for both bank and insurance company counties. But bank and insurance companies differ sharply with respect to the relative importance of dairy as compared with crop and livestock farming. In the third and fourth quartiles, however, bank and insurance company groupings differ sharply from one another with respect to both criteria. It is probable that individuals finance relatively more of the low-cropland agriculture in the Central states than in the older sections of the East and South.

Despite the roughness of some of the data from which the foregoing comparisons have been drawn, they do indicate that sources of credit are related to characteristics of agriculture. These characteristics, in turn, appear to influence the distribution of operator and landlord interests in agricultural assets. Counties in which investment by banks and individuals is heaviest are characterized also by high operator interests, and those in which land bank and insurance company investment is greatest, by high landlord interests. Contrasts are most clear, in this respect, between the bank and the insurance company counties. The bank counties appear to include those where specialization in capital provision as such is rather limited. The farm operator provides most of the equity capital, and local lenders, who are likely to participate also in general managerial decisions, provide debt capital. On the other hand, the insurance company group includes counties in which the two functions—capital provision and responsibility taking—frequently are performed by separate investors. Here absentee landlords are likely to be the principal sources of equity capital, while debt capital tends to come largely from centralized lenders who participate little in general managerial decisions.

Four Non-Real-Estate Lenders

Four major credit agencies extended non-real-estate credit to agriculture in 1940. These were commercial banks, Production Credit Associations, the Farm Security Administration, and the Emergency Crop and Feed Loan Division of the Farm Credit Administration, and their objectives were so different that one would expect them to have served fairly distinct credit markets. Their functional specialization may be revealed if we select from the 108 counties, separately for each of the lender groups, the 36 in which the ratio of non-real-estate bank loans to total non-real-estate assets was highest, and then compare the four resulting sets of counties to determine differences in economic and financial characteristics (Table 31).

It may be observed that all four groups of counties in Table 31 have common characteristics. As compared with the sample as a whole, all had moderately high land-to-asset ratios and were somewhat more heavily engaged in crop and livestock production. None of the four groups was intensively engaged in dairy production. On the financial side, all four were characterized by higher-than-average creditor interests and lower-than-average operator interests. But with the exception of the bank counties, their farms were smaller than average.

Among the groups we find greater similarity than might be expected, probably because each group contains counties with quite diverse characteristics. For example, the PCA counties include small-farm counties of the Southeast and large livestock farm counties of the West. Similarly, among the counties characterized by heavy Emergency Crop and Feed loans there are small-farm counties of the Southeast and large grain farms of the Great Plains. It is likely, moreover, that the economic indicators used in this study are not particularly well adapted to an analysis of functional specialization among short-term credit agencies. More marked differences among the four groups of counties might well emerge if it were possible to compare yield variations attributable to natural hazards.[4]

To test the significance of the financial experience factor, Table 32 presents a separate analysis by asset-deflation classes. In general, the pattern of farm asset size relationship shown in Table 31 holds also within asset-deflation classes. The nine counties in which bank loans are highest in relation to non-real-estate assets are characterized by larger farms than the counties in which PCA loans are highest, whereas the FSA counties are characterized by lower farm asset size than either the bank or the PCA counties. The higher-than-average level of farm asset size in ECFL counties in the first quartile (most severe asset defla-

---

[4] Other possible explanations of the lack of differentiation are: (1) While the extent of credit requirements is influenced by the economic characteristics of agriculture, the sources from which the credit is drawn are determined by other considerations. (2) Federal agencies do actually serve a broad credit market; they made loans both to farms for which credit was not available from private credit institutions and to farms which had been financed earlier by private agencies but were now in distress.

TABLE 31

ECONOMIC AND FINANCIAL CHARACTERISTICS:

Four Groups of 36 Counties in Which Non-Real-Estate Loans of a Specified Type Were Highest in Relation to Total Non-Real-Estate Assets

(dollar figures in thousands)

	Banks	PCA's	FSA	ECFL Division of FCA	108 Counties
Ratio of non-real-estate loans of lender group to total non-real-estate assets[a]	19%	6%	10%	8%	....
Economic Characteristics					
Physical assets per farm	$9.8	$6.7	$5.2	$6.5	$8.3
Physical assets in:					
Land	59%	56%	54%	56%	52%
Buildings	19	20	21	20	23
Non-real-estate	22	24	25	24	25
Cropland/total acreage[b]	44	34	35	40	40
Dwellings/farm real estate, 1930	15	15	17	16	16
Farm product value, 1939:					
Crops and livestock	70	71	64	69	63
Dairy products	8	6	9	7	13
Poultry and prod. and misc.	5	5	5	4	6
Used by farm household	17	18	22	20	18
Off-farm work in days, 1939[c]	29	34	32	30	35
Change in phys. asset value, 1930-1940[d]	−23%	−22%	−24%	−24%	−22%
Financial Characteristics					
Interest in physical assets of:					
Operators	42%	44%	45%	43%	48%
Landlords	32	32	28	31	29
Creditors	26	24	27	26	23
Mtgd. farms/all farms	45	43	42	44	43
Mtg. debt/value of mtgd. farms	39	37	40	40	40
Mtg. debt/value of all farms	19	18	18	18	19
Farm mtg. debt held by:					
FLB's and FFMC	49	48	54	59	47
Ins. and mtg. investment companies	19	14	11	8	12
Commercial and savings banks	9	9	8	8	10
Individuals and miscellaneous	23	29	27	25	31
Non-real-estate loans of four lender groups as % of total non-real-estate farm assets	31	24	34	32	21

(footnotes on next page)

Footnotes to Table 31

ᵃ Counties were selected so that each group had, on the average, about the same degree of asset deflation in the 1930's.

ᵇ Cropland excludes plowable pasture.

ᶜ Per farm operator.

ᵈ The four groups of counties are compared below with the respective groups based on a straight array of counties without regard to asset deflation.

	Banks	PCA's	FSA	ECFL Division of FCA
Change in physical asset values, 1930-1940	−24%	−17%	−24%	−30%
Non-real-estate loans/non-real-estate assets	19	6	10	9

tion) is explained by the fact that this group includes a number of large cash grain counties in the Great Plains.

The tendency for land to run high as a percentage of total assets in all four groups of 36 counties in Table 31 is corroborated by the breakdown in Table 32. Of the 16 comparisons by this criterion only two show the land-assets ratio (98 and 94 respectively) to be below the average for the 27-county group with which the nine are compared.

Similar comparisons based on the ratio of cropland to total acreage bring out certain contrasts that are obscured in the averages shown for the 36-county groups in Table 31. The PCA and FSA counties in the first quartile (greatest asset deflation) are characterized by a low ratio of cropland to total acreage, which reflects the tendency of both credit agencies to lend to livestock farms in these areas. In the fourth quartile, however, which includes a large number of the smaller crop farms of the South, cropland is at least as important in the PCA and FSA counties as in the entire 27-county group. Furthermore, in both the first and fourth quartiles, the Emergency Crop and Feed Loan Division made most of its loans in counties that ranked high by cropland component acreage. Drought conditions accounted for many of these loans to farms in counties included in the first quartile, whereas in the fourth quartile ECFL financing represents more regular production loans to farmers who could not qualify for credit with other agencies. The separate breakdown by asset-deflation classes serves mainly to illustrate the tendency of these federally sponsored credit sources to lend to diverse kinds of agriculture.

In Table 33 (based on data from Tables 30 and 32) we may seek evidence of complementary relationships between banks

TABLE 32

ECONOMIC CHARACTERISTICS:

Nine Counties with Highest Ratio of Non-Real-Estate Loans of a Specified Type of Lender to Total Non-Real-Estate Assets Compared with Quartile Groups of Counties Ranked by Asset Deflation

	NINE COUNTIES WITH HIGHEST RATIOS OF NON-REAL-ESTATE LOANS OF SPECIFIED TYPE OF LENDER TO TOTAL NON-REAL-ESTATE ASSETS (AVG. FOR RESPECTIVE QUARTILE GROUP = 100)				
	Asset-Deflation Quartiles[a]				Average of Quartiles
ECONOMIC CHARACTERISTICS AND LENDER GROUP	1st	2nd	3rd	4th	
Physical assets per farm					
Banks	119	97	141	122	120
PCA's	114	67	77	91	87
FSA	95	53	68	50	67
ECFL Division of FCA	104	80	71	77	83
Land in % of total physical assets					
Banks	112	112	128	100	113
PCA's	110	98	113	103	106
FSA	108	106	111	94	105
ECFL Division of FCA	107	112	116	103	109
Cropland in % of total acreage					
Banks	96	116	109	103	106
PCA's	61	85	87	111	86
FSA	66	88	80	100	84
ECFL Division of FCA	119	85	78	116	100
Sales of crops and livestock in % of total value of product					
Banks	107	111	121	105	111
PCA's	120	99	118	113	112
FSA	111	102	100	92	101
ECFL Division of FCA	111	106	111	106	108
Sales of dairy products in % of total value of product					
Banks	66	48	65	77	64
PCA's	50	62	49	26	47
FSA	58	55	65	100	70
ECFL Division of FCA	66	62	43	38	52

[a] The 108 counties were arrayed by degree of asset deflation in the 1930's, from greatest to least, and divided into quartiles. For each quartile the nine counties with the highest ratios of non-real-estate loans of specified lender groups to total non-real-estate assets are compared with the average for the quartile group as a whole in this respect.

TABLE 33

ECONOMIC CHARACTERISTICS:

Nine Counties with the Highest Specified Credit Ratios Compared with Quartile Groups of Counties Ranked by Asset Deflation

FINANCIAL RATIO AND ECO-NOMIC CHARACTERISTICS	NINE COUNTIES WITH HIGHEST SPECIFIED CREDIT RATIOS (AVG. FOR RESPECTIVE QUARTILE GROUP = 100)				
	Asset-Deflation Quartiles[a]				Average of Quartiles
	1st	2nd	3rd	4th	
Mtg. loans of ins. and mtg. inv. cos./total farm real estate assets					
Physical assets per farm	124	120	117	144	126
Land in % of total physical assets	107	114	121	112	113
Cropland in % of total acreage	115	130	120	146	128
Sales of crops and livestock in % of total value of product, 1939	104	107	126	120	114
Sales of dairy products in % of total value of product, 1939	78	67	50	42	59
Non-real-estate loans of banks/total non-real-estate farm assets					
Physical assets per farm	119	97	141	122	120
Land in % of total physical assets	112	112	128	100	113
Cropland in % of total acreage	96	116	109	103	106
Sales of crops and livestock in % of total value of product, 1939	107	111	121	105	111
Sales of dairy products in % of total value of product, 1939	66	48	65	77	64
Mtg. loans of banks/total real estate farm assets					
Physical assets per farm	112	99	107	47	92
Land in % of total physical assets	93	84	73	88	85
Cropland in % of total acreage	115	123	91	71	100
Sales of crops and livestock in % of total value of product, 1939	89	84	81	87	85
Sales of dairy products in % of total value of product, 1939	157	160	157	82	139

[a] The 108 counties were arrayed by degree of asset deflation in the 1930's, from greatest to least, and divided into quartiles. For each quartile the nine counties that were highest with respect to specified credit ratios are compared with the average for the quartile group as a whole in this respect.

137

as sources of non-real-estate funds and insurance companies as sources of real estate funds. Here it is possible also to compare the kinds of agriculture in which banks' non-real-estate loans run highest in relation to non-real-estate assets with the kinds in which their real estate loans run highest in relation to real estate assets. High mortgage loan ratios of insurance companies and high non-real-estate loan ratios of banks are found to coexist in counties characterized by low sales of dairy products and high crop and livestock production, as well as by a high land component of total assets. But the parallels are less clear in comparisons based on asset size of farm and cropland component of acreage.

The contrasts between counties in which the non-real-estate loans of banks run high and those in which their real estate loans run high are fairly sharp. It is possible that the difference is due in part to the nature of the security required for loans rather than to the kinds of agriculture banks finance. For example, in agriculture with a strong representation of landlord investment and insurance company loans, real estate is less frequently available as security for intermediate-term loans. On the other hand, where the operator owns the real estate assets as well as the non-real-estate assets, banks may make loans more frequently for production purposes with the real estate as supplemental security.

CHAPTER 7

SUMMARY: THE ROLE OF CREDIT IN THE CAPITAL STRUCTURE OF AGRICULTURE

WHILE the data presented in the foregoing chapters lend considerable support to the original hypothesis that particular combinations of asset and product patterns may influence the capital structure of farms, they provide only a cross-section view for a single year. Before we summarize the main conclusions drawn from these data it may be appropriate, therefore, to discuss briefly one of the chief limitations of a cross-section approach to this study, namely the impact of previous financial experience on farm capital structure and credit use.

The net effect of the severe asset deflation that occurred during the 1930's was to bring about an erosion of ownership interests in assets, and thus to cause creditor interests to appear more important in 1940 than they would if farm credit structure were viewed on a long-run historical basis. On the other hand, asset inflation in the 1940's served to increase disproportionately the interests of equity holders. Such distortions are especially serious when considerable increases or decreases are reflected in the market values of farm assets, whether or not these assets have actually changed hands.

The relative increase in creditor interests that would normally occur during a period of moderate asset deflation may be strenghened by a concurrent rise in the amount of farm credit outstanding. An increase in indebtedness is most likely to occur on farms with a substantial cushion of owner equity; on the other hand, if the equity cushion is too small, or if asset and income deflation are unusually severe, a rise in foreclosures will transform creditor interests into owner equities. These opposing influences are modified also by the extension of credit through governmental agencies to farmers in financial distress. Comparisons among counties that are similar in type of agriculture but differ greatly in the extent of financial difficulties experienced in the 1930's indicate that the net effect of severe asset deflation was, in most cases, to raise the creditor interest in farm assets relative to its level in counties that suffered only moderate asset deflation.[1]

[1] During a period of asset inflation a high level of farm income may permit an abnormally accelerated rate of debt retirement and in this way supplement

Finally, the effect on farm capital structure of longer-run financial changes like those of the 1930's can be seen also in the distribution of farm debt as between long- and short-term obligations and among different lender groups. Long-term debts are not only less responsive to adjustment than short-term debts, but the latter may be transformed into the former by a refinancing operation, which would tend, at the end of a period of asset deflation, to make the use of long-term debt funds appear to be especially heavy in those areas where asset deflation was most severe. Here again, of course, the precise outcome will reflect also the effects of lending policies adopted by government credit agencies.

In short, previous financial experience and the lending operations of government agencies leave their traces on the pattern of farm capital structure, viewed at the end of a period of falling asset values. These traces becloud such evidence as may point to the influence of specific agricultural characteristics. The procedures adopted in this study for taking account of the effect of differences in financial experience are designed to reduce the influence of this factor, but they cannot, of course, eliminate it. This fact, therefore, the reader should bear in mind as, in the following sections, we present a summary of findings in response to these questions: (1) How do the economic characteristics of a given type of agriculture affect its use of outside financing? (2) What is the effect of these characteristics upon the extent to which outside financing is acquired in the form of debt? and (3) What factors influence the extent to which different sources of credit are drawn upon for farm financing?

Factors Affecting Outside Investment in Farms

One of the basic economic factors that governs the demand for outside financing—that is, financing other than that provided directly by the farm operator—appears to be the asset size of the farm unit. In view of the limited capacity of most farm operators to accumulate capital out of their own income, needs for outside financing tend to rise with farm size. This does not mean that asset size is unaffected by the availability of outside capital. What we assume is that major differences in asset size

---

the effect that such a broad change has on financial structure. To the extent that new debts are incurred to acquire farms at higher levels of land prices, the tendency for asset inflation to lower the debt-to-equity ratio may be offset, but this would be true only for those farms that actually changed hands.

140

occur independently of capital availability, and that if farms of large asset size have distinct investment advantages over small units, outside capital will ordinarily become available to them in one form or another.

A number of other factors, in addition to asset size, influence the extent to which outside funds will be used and the sources from which these funds will be drawn. Previous financial experience of an area has a demonstrable effect on credit use, as have also those economic characteristics that bear on the attractiveness of farm property as loan security, or as a channel for ownership investment by nonoperators. Moreover, where asset size is large but there is a lack of features that would make the property attractive to conventional outside investors, higher-than-average operator interests will be needed, or special arrangements that combine nonoperator ownership with responsible hired management will have to be made. The corporate form of organization may be most appropriate where production and marketing efficiency demands unusually large asset size but where neither creditor investment nor conventional individual equity investment can be obtained in sufficient volume.

While it is possible to identify a substantial range of combinations of agricultural characteristics that would both require and be attractive to outside sources of capital, and another set that would tend in the opposite direction, the data on 108 counties permit the drawing of at least an average profile of features that affect demand for outside financing. Such profiles are given in Table 34 in the form of averages based on the 36 counties in which farms drew the highest, and the 36 counties in which they drew the lowest, proportions of their capital funds from outside sources.

The first group, which relied for almost two thirds of its capital on outside sources, is comprised of counties with farms that are more than 50 per cent larger, on the average, than farms in the second group, which drew only about three eighths of its capital from outside. Furthermore, farms in the first 36 counties are characterized by higher-than-average ratios of land to total physical assets and of cropland to total acreage, and by a higher-than-average product throw-off in the form of cash crops and livestock. These asset and product characteristics appear to be of the kind that encourage and facilitate the investment of outside funds.

141

TABLE 34

ECONOMIC AND FINANCIAL CHARACTERISTICS IN RELATION TO:

Outside Interest in Farm Assets, High and Low Thirds of 108 Counties

(dollars in thousands)

ECONOMIC AND FINANCIAL CHARACTERISTICS	COUNTY GROUP	
	36 with Highest Outside Interest	36 with Lowest Outside Interest[a]
Interest of outside investors in physical assets	65%	37%
Economic Characteristics		
Physical assets per farm	$10.1	$6.6
Physical assets in:		
Land	61%	43%
Buildings	16	31
Non-real-estate	23	26
Cropland/total acreage[b]	46	36
Dwellings/farm real estate, 1930	12	21
Farm product value, 1939:		
Crops and livestock	76	47
Dairy products	7	23
Poultry and prod. and misc.	3	10
Used by farm household	14	20
Off-farm work in days, 1939[c]	26	49
Change in phys. asset value, 1930-1940[d]	−23%	−22%
Financial Characteristics		
Interest in physical assets of:		
Operators	35%	63%
Landlords	38	18
Creditors	27	19
Mtgd. farms/all farms	47	41
Mtg. debt/value of mtgd. farms	41	41
Mtg. debt/value of all farms	21	18
Farm mtg. debt held by:		
FLB's and FFMC	52	43
Ins. and mtg. investment companies	17	8
Commercial and savings banks	6	12
Individuals and miscellaneous	25	37
Non-real-estate loans, as % of total non-real-estate farm assets, of:		
Banks and PCA's	18	9
FSA and ECFL Division of FCA	11	4

[a] Outside interest includes landlord and creditor interests.

[b] Cropland excludes plowable pasture.

[c] Per farm operator.

(footnotes concluded on next page)

142

Footnotes to Table 34 (concluded)

d The following tabulation, based on a straight array of counties, permits a comparison of the interest of outside investors with that shown above:

	High 36	Low 36
Interest of outside investors	67%	36%
Change in phys. assets, 1930-1940	—31	—21

It should be recalled, however, that the specific combination of farm characteristics revealed by the averages for these counties is only one of several such combinations that would attract substantial outside investment. As might be expected, fairly high outside interests are found in types of agriculture where moderate over-all capital requirements per farm are combined with features that are unusually attractive to outside investors. On the other hand, counties with very small farms seldom show high outside interests even when other characteristics of the agriculture appear favorable.

Although this study cannot provide precise formulas for estimating the "normal" proportion of outside interests in a sector of agriculture, it may point the way for fruitful research in this direction. The amount of outside interest in farm assets is the result of the interaction of market influences which can be classified broadly into "demand" and "supply" categories. Important factors lying back of the demand for capital to supplement that which the farm operator himself can furnish are technological and marketing influences that determine the most efficient size of unit in a particular kind of farming. Whether large-sized units will be financed more or less heavily with outside funds, and what sources will supply them, will depend mainly on the characteristics of the agriculture. These characteristics can be grouped broadly with those connected with asset composition and those associated with nature of the product and the productive process.

Fully to understand the nature of the capital supply responses of different types of potential outside investors in agriculture, and to appraise their significance for different sectors of the agricultural economy, would require an independent study of the institutional arrangements through which capital flows to agriculture. The largest gap in our knowledge in this respect relates not to credit institutions but to individual lenders and nonoperating owners of farms, a group of capital suppliers that greatly exceeds in importance the combined public and private credit institutions which lend to agriculture. This gap will have to be filled before we can define with precision the role of outside financing in agriculture.

Distribution of Total Outside Interests by Investor Groups

What forces determine the division of outside farm investment as between debt and equity funds? And what forces determine how total farm credit in use is apportioned among different types of lenders? We cannot answer such questions categorically, though the data analyzed in this study throw some light on the influences that bear upon them.

The first general observation that can be made concerning the relation between debt and nonoperator equity is that debt as a component of outside financing tends to be heaviest among farms of smaller-than-average size. The fact that landlord investment is not usually attracted to these farms means that their needs for outside financing, modest as they are for the individual unit, will be satisfied largely on a creditorship basis. The loan contract seems to be a more effective device than the real estate lease in providing this type of agriculture with the additional capital required.

Second, it appears that whether or not the creditor interest in large farms is a greater-than-average percentage of total outside interest depends in part on the nature of the agriculture involved. Some large farms, thanks to their asset patterns and their agricultural operations, can attract enough equity investment on the part of nonoperators to make a large volume of credit unnecessary. Other forms of farm enterprise may be less attractive to nonoperating equity investors but can nevertheless provide adequate security for higher-than-average amounts of debt funds. The total credit used depends, of course, on the separate amounts of real estate credit and non-real-estate credit employed; these, in turn, are apparently governed by somewhat different sets of circumstances.

Third, landlord investment tends to be a more variable element in farm financial structure than creditor investment. Thus, as can be observed in Table 34, in the counties most heavily dependent on outside funds landlord investment constituted 38 per cent of the total funds used, and in those least dependent only 18 per cent, whereas creditor investment in the same county groups was 27 and 19 per cent, respectively. This may be explained in part by the fact that often where mortgage credit is not used extensively, a greater-than-average amount of non-real-estate credit may be employed, so that the credit ingredient in total outside financing remains relatively constant. Moreover, contracts, regardless of the basis for the loans, may vary so widely in terms and conditions that debt funds bearing a given ratio to total assets can represent investments ranging from the equivalent of high-grade bonds to near-equity commitments. Creditor investment is adaptable to widely different circumstances, a characteristic which would tend to invalidate sweeping generalizations regarding the kinds of agriculture that use much or little credit.

When each type of debt—mortgage and non-real-estate—is considered separately in relation, respectively, to total real estate assets and total non-real-estate assets, certain meaningful relationships are found, although it must be borne in mind that credit secured by real estate may be used to finance non-real-estate assets.

A high 1940 ratio of real estate debt to real estate assets may reflect mainly the unfavorable financial experience of a county in the 1930's, but it may also result from varying combinations of the following circumstances:

1. Asset requirements per farm so high as to require substantial outside investment, a larger-than-average part of which may take the form of real estate loans
2. Farm assets or products (or both) of types that militate against absentee ownership because of high risks or high supervisory costs (or both)
3. Real estate assets and the kinds of production that are considered appropriate as loan security

No one of these sets of circumstances taken separately, however, can be expected to result in higher-than-average use of real estate credit. For example, unusually high asset requirements per farm in a kind of agriculture that is also unusually attractive to equity investment by nonoperators may not result in high real estate debt even though the property may be excellent security for such credit. Furthermore, agriculture in which asset and product characteristics tend to dampen landlord investment may also have farm units so small that little real estate credit is needed to supplement the capital funds that can be provided by the operator. Such agriculture may also be considered to be inadequate security for real estate loans by most lenders.[2]

Some of the western wheat and range livestock counties appear to represent a still different combination of these factors. Here total asset requirements are high, but production risks are so great that both landlords and creditors are deterred from extensive investment. Such agriculture may attract as operators a larger-than-average proportion of farmers with substantial funds of their own. Thus the proportion of total real estate that is represented by real estate loans in these counties may be smaller than in other counties with lower asset requirements per farm but otherwise better suited to creditor investment.

One combination of circumstances that results in extensive use of real estate credit is illustrated by moderately large, commercial dairy and general farms with a high cropland component of total acreage. The size of these farms calls for substantial amounts of outside investment, and the nature of their operations and other characteristics of their assets tend to discourage equity investment by nonoperators. Nevertheless, a high cropland component of total acreage apparently constitutes a basis for real estate loans in substantial volume. But where smaller asset requirements prevail, or where the real estate is less satisfactory as loan security, there is less tendency toward heavy use of real estate credit. A study of individual-county comparisons suggests also that as the product of moderately large units becomes more heavily weighted with cash-crop farming, increased investment by nonoperating owners tends to reduce the use of real estate credit.

High non-real-estate loans in relation to non-real-estate assets, in contrast to high real estate loan ratios, tend to accompany high landlord investment. This latter structural characteristic of financing is well illustrated by large-scale, cash-crop agriculture, and the explanation probably lies in the relative ease with which landlord investment can be managed. Heavy seasonal expenses and substantial per farm investment in machinery and equipment, which characterize this type of agriculture, frequently compel tenant operators to borrow a substantial part of their operating capital on security other than real estate. Furthermore, insurance companies and specialized land credit institutions pro-

[2] This does not necessarily mean that agriculture in such areas could not be reorganized so that the resulting larger units would be more attractive to investment by nonoperators; these farms also would need more credit to supplement equity funds.

vide a large part of the real estate credit used in such agriculture, so that operating capital tends to be financed with non-real-estate loans. This specialization in agricultural lending is in contrast to the real estate loans with which local lenders frequently finance both working capital and land purchase requirements in other kinds of agriculture.

The data on which this study is based are not very well adapted to a detailed analysis of relationships between the economic characteristics of agriculture and the use of non-real-estate credit. Such evidence as is available suggests that the use of non-real-estate credit is not determined solely by the amount of non-real-estate assets employed in farming. Indeed the use of non-real-estate credit may be moderate even where non-real-estate assets bulk very large in total farm assets. This appears to be the case in dairy farming, for example, and may be due partly to the tendency to use real estate loans to finance permanent working capital assets such as herds and equipment and partly also to a less-than-average need for seasonal financing.

It does not follow that in an agriculture of such a nature that specialized land-credit agencies offer real estate loans on attractive terms, farmers will finance their operating capital needs from the same source. Indeed, the likelihood is that they will borrow on a non-real-estate basis from a local lender for this purpose. But where the bulk of real estate credit is provided locally, specialization of lending by type of security is less likely to be observed. Here the local lender may cover both long- and short-term credit needs under the single security of real estate. It is probable, therefore, that the influence of the economic characteristics of agriculture on non-real-estate credit use is rather indirect.

Perhaps the most general explanation for heavy dependence on debt financing is to be sought less in the acceptability of the security offered than in a combination of circumstances that leaves a wider-than-average gap between total capital requirements per farm and the combined equity investment that operators are able, and landlords are willing, to make.[3] Differences in the importance of credit in farm capital structures cannot

[3] The point should be reemphasized that the "gap" in equity capital supply referred to here is one that would normally be expected to be present even though agriculture did not experience prolonged periods of deflation or inflation. In a period of prolonged low farm income, greater credit use by some farms might be explained in part in terms of a continuing gap between receipts and necessary current outlays, which would necessitate additional

be fully explained except in terms of over-all capital needs of individual farms, on the one hand, and the effectiveness of the agricultural capital market in providing equity capital, on the other. If this approach is valid, it becomes impossible adequately to analyze the role of credit in farm financing without also analyzing the role of equity financing by both operators and non-operators.

Agency Specialization in Farm Financing

Finally, we may turn to a summary of the factors that appear to influence the extent to which mortgage credit and short- and intermediate-term production credit are drawn from each of the principal sources.

Farms differ perhaps most widely in the degree to which they draw long-term credit funds on a mortgage basis from local sources. The extent of this difference is indicated by levels of the ratio of farm mortgage loans held by banks, individuals, and other local lenders to total real estate assets. Where this ratio is high, the agriculture is usually such that administration costs of absentee lenders, as well as investment management costs of absentee landlords, also are high. Specifically, it is an agriculture characterized by a large buildings component of real estate assets, and by greater-than-average livestock, machinery, and other non-real-estate components of total assets. The product pattern also tends to be more consistently associated with kinds of farming operations that rely heavily for their success on proper day-to-day management decisions.

In agriculture of this type, farm operators ordinarily furnish a considerable part of the total farm capital. It is a kind of farming in which the functions of capital provision, responsibility taking, and management tend to overlap but to remain within the province of the operator himself. Lenders find it necessary to protect their interests as capital suppliers in such agriculture by taking careful account of the competence and character of the borrower as well as of the security offered.

The fact that as of 1940 there was no observable tendency toward specialization in the lending activities of the federal land

---

borrowing to cover operating losses. Likewise, in a period of rapidly rising farm asset prices, those who buy farms might have to use more credit to pay for them. The need for additional credit in these two contrasting situations is related more to changing economic conditions than to long-run characteristics of farms as units of economic organization or to long-run characteristics of the capital market for agriculture.

banks or the Federal Farm Mortgage Corporation probably reflects the widespread refinancing they undertook in the 1930's. Insurance companies, on the other hand, appear to fit into a fairly distinct functional niche. Loans by such companies ran highest in relation to real estate assets in agriculture characterized by larger-than-average assets per farm, by a high land component of total assets, and by a high cash-crop component of total sales.

In general, the insurance company appears to have been less deterred as a mortgagee by farming risks arising from variations in price and yield than by those arising from differences in management ability. Loans from this source are highest in agriculture characterized by a high degree of specialization in the functions of capital provision, responsibility taking, and management. The function of providing equity capital is concentrated to a greater extent than elsewhere in the hands of absentee real estate owners; mortgage credit is furnished largely by the insurance companies, and non-real-estate credit mainly by banks and PCA's. Responsibility taking is divided between operators and landlords, and the management function is in the main the special role of the operator. Agriculture in which capital provision can be divorced in this way from management and responsibility taking can obtain more of its capital from a broad, outside capital market than can agriculture in which the lender must assume at least a supervisory managerial function.

The areas in which insurance company loans and landlord equities are highest are not identical: both tend to be low where farms are small and management is an important factor. But whereas insurance company loans are also low where uncertainty arising from price and yield variation is great, a high level of landlord investment is frequently maintained even in this type of agriculture. Insurance companies as lenders are unable—because of their organizational basis, their commitments to policyholders, and the state supervisory systems under which they operate—to take large risks with the expectation that high farm earnings in years of good yields and prices will offset defaults in years of low yields and prices. Indeed, the mortgage contract is such that they can get little if any benefit from high farm earnings except a more rapid pay-off of loans, while they can suffer severe loss from low earnings and the resultant defaults. Landlords, being equity investors, are better able to take such risks because they have an opportunity, especially under share leases, to participate in the high earnings of years of good yields and prices and also to profit from the sale of the farm if real estate values should rise.

Specialization on the part of the four types of non-real-estate lenders is somewhat more difficult to discern. The kinds of agriculture in which FSA and Emergency Crop and Feed Loan Division credits were highest in relation to non-real-estate assets in 1940 varied in terms of the economic distress which these public agencies were organized to relieve. As for PCA's and commercial banks, the data in this study indicate few clear-cut differences in the types of farming served by them. There is some evidence that production loans of commercial banks are highest in relation to non-real-estate assets in the same type of agriculture in which landlord investment and insurance company mortgage lending are highest. Mortgage loans of commercial banks, on the other hand, appear to run highest in relation to real estate assets where operator investment is high and where there is but a limited use of non-real-estate credit.

Thus, where landlords and insurance companies are important as suppliers of long-term capital, commercial banks fit into the financial picture mainly as suppliers of non-real-estate credit. But where equity capital for real estate ownership is supplied mainly by the operator and by local individuals, banks tend to participate more as mortgage lenders. In short, banks appear to adjust their agricultural lending to the capital supply situation prevailing in any area. The net result is a complementary relationship between commercial banks and other sources of farm capital, although in such instances of specialization as have been noted, competitive conditions rather than preferences in risk selection may be the controlling factor.

Concluding Observations

What then is the distinctive role of credit in the capital structure of agriculture? It is difficult to find a description of this role that is at once broad enough to embrace all situations and specific enough to have real meaning. Thus, if credit plays a distinctive part in agricultural capital structure, this fact probably stems directly from the essential nature of the debtor-creditor relationship, which permits a wider separation than almost any other form of investment between the capital provision and responsibility-taking functions. Phrased differently, through the instrumentality of credit, capital can be invested without the investors' assuming a proportionate share of the risks of the enterprise being

150

financed. By the same token, the farmer can obtain capital without sharing control over the farm business. While such a definition of the role of credit helps to explain why credit is useful to individual borrowers and lenders, it does not assign any distinctive role to credit in agricultural finance.

In this study we have been more concerned with the question as to why credit is more important in the financing of one kind of agriculture than in the financing of another. The explanation is found in part, but only in part, in the relative attractiveness of different kinds of agriculture as security. Only when the use of credit is related also to those characteristics of agriculture which tend to attract nonoperator equity investment do we encounter a plausible explanation for variations in credit use. Unfortunately, this is precisely the sector of the agricultural capital market about which we have the least knowledge. When we can assemble information on individual lenders and nonoperating investors of farm equity capital to supplement our knowledge of credit institutions, we shall be better able to define the role of credit in farm financing.

Summary Table

	PERCENTAGE CHANGE IN PHYSICAL ASSET VALUE, 1930-1940	DISTRIBUTION OF PHYSICAL ASSET VALUE				DWELLINGS A A PER CENT OF FARM REAL ESTATE VALUE, 1930
		Land & Build- ings	Land	Build- ings	Non- Real- Estate Assets	
Range Livestock Counties						
Tom Green, Texas	+18.6%	81%	73%	8%	19%	6%
Catron, New Mexico	+5.0	66	57	9	34	5
Webb, Texas	−3.1	79	75	4	21	3
Carter, Oklahoma	−7.6	77	62	15	23	15
Siskiyou, California	−15.6	74	58	16	26	9
Yavapai, Arizona	−23.1	66	53	13	34	8
Brewster, Texas	−24.7	77	74	3	23	2
Chautauqua, Kansas	−26.2	73	58	14	28	12
Elko, Nevada	−28.7	54	46	8	46	7
San Miguel, New Mexico	−35.8	70	59	10	30	7
Union, Oregon	−41.6	78	61	17	22	11
Custer, Montana	−42.6	67	54	14	33	8
Union, New Mexico	−45.7	70	63	7	31	5
Dawes, Nebraska	−45.9	73	59	14	27	9
Haakon, South Dakota	−59.4	65	54	11	35	8
Corn Belt Counties						
Daviess, Kentucky	−7.2	80	55	25	20	16
Wayne, Indiana	−9.1	79	45	34	21	20
Putnam, Ohio	−10.7	80	52	29	20	15
Douglas, Illinois	−10.8	84	71	13	16	7
Calhoun, Michigan	−16.5	72	34	38	28	28
Green, Wisconsin	−24.9	66	33	33	34	18
Stark, Illinois	−30.3	83	65	18	16	9
Hamilton, Iowa	−32.4	81	60	20	19	10
Cherokee, Iowa	−34.2	78	57	20	22	8
Appanoose, Iowa	−43.9	68	48	20	32	14
Day, South Dakota	−47.4	72	47	25	28	12
Cass, Missouri	−48.2	76	51	25	24	14
Pierce, Nebraska	−55.4	74	56	19	26	9
Franklin, Nebraska	−62.6	76	59	17	24	10
Eastern Cotton Counties						
Jenkins, Georgia	+14.4	77	53	24	23	19
Dillon, South Carolina	+12.7	84	61	23	16	19
Edgecombe, North Carolina	+8.2	82	54	28	18	19
Gordon, Georgia	+3.1	79	56	23	21	19
Warren, Mississippi	−4.1	75	53	22	25	23
Hardeman, Tennessee	−5.1	74	53	21	26	24
Greene, Georgia	−6.4	72	44	28	28	32
Wilcox, Georgia	−9.7	76	53	23	24	19
Lee, Alabama	−11.4	76	52	24	24	25
Kershaw, South Carolina	−11.5	77	51	26	23	19
Tishomingo, Mississippi	−20.2	73	52	21	27	23
Etowah, Alabama	−24.1	79	57	22	21	12
Lowndes, Alabama	−24.9	68	43	25	32	20
Coahoma, Mississippi	−9.1	87	70	17	13	16
Lauderdale, Mississippi	−32.1	77	47	30	23	31

(continued on next page)

Summary Table (continued)

| | PERCENTAGE CHANGE IN PHYSICAL ASSET VALUE, 1930-1940 | DISTRIBUTION OF PHYSICAL ASSET VALUE | | | | DWELLINGS AS A PER CENT OF FARM REAL ESTATE VALUE, 1930 |
		Land & Buildings	Land	Buildings	Non-Real-Estate Assets	
Western Cotton Counties						
Crittenden, Arkansas	+15.8%	85%	68%	17%	15%	13%
Tyler, Texas	+11.1	79	48	31	21	29
Chicot, Arkansas	+5.2	79	62	17	21	19
Upshur, Texas	−6.5	79	55	24	21	26
Natchitoches, Louisiana	−13.3	76	58	18	24	17
Lubbock, Texas	−14.3	83	69	14	17	10
St. Landry, Louisiana	−14.7	73	55	18	27	17
Nolan, Texas	−19.3	80	69	11	20	8
Cleveland, Oklahoma	−20.9	82	67	15	18	13
Young, Texas	−26.2	82	70	12	18	9
Bradley, Arkansas	−26.4	73	49	24	27	26
Burleson, Texas	−27.0	79	63	16	21	13
Washita, Oklahoma	−31.6	81	68	13	19	9
Kaufman, Texas	−39.4	82	68	14	18	12
DeWitt, Texas	−40.7	77	57	20	23	13
Wheat Belt Counties						
Adams, Washington	−8.3	82	74	8	18	6
Polk, Minnesota	−16.2	71	47	23	29	14
Garfield, Oklahoma	−21.3	80	69	11	19	8
Hill, Montana	−28.5	71	59	12	29	7
Hansford, Texas	−34.7	81	74	8	18	4
Rush, Kansas	−38.3	85	75	10	14	6
Cheyenne, Nebraska	−40.8	80	66	14	20	7
Williams, North Dakota	−46.2	75	56	19	25	13
Day, South Dakota	−47.4	68	48	20	32	12
Benson, North Dakota	−49.9	69	48	21	31	11
Hettinger, North Dakota	−50.6	73	55	18	27	10
Decatur, Kansas	−51.8	82	68	14	18	8
Logan, Kansas	−56.9	80	70	10	20	5
Franklin, Nebraska	−62.6	76	59	17	24	10
Hyde, South Dakota	−63.8	56	40	16	44	8
Western Dairy Counties						
Koochiching, Minnesota	+.7	70	43	26	31	18
Alpena, Michigan	+6.1	66	35	31	34	25
Sanilac, Michigan	−3.8	65	33	32	35	22
Shiawassee, Michigan	−13.8	71	33	37	29	25
Polk, Minnesota	−16.2	71	48	23	29	14
Winnebago, Wisconsin	−15.6	69	35	34	31	21
Calhoun, Michigan	−16.5	72	34	38	28	28
Green, Wisconsin	−24.9	66	33	33	34	18
Wood, Wisconsin	−29.9	66	30	37	34	20
Meeker, Minnesota	−31.7	69	40	29	31	15
Ashland, Wisconsin	−33.5	62	31	31	38	22
Winona, Minnesota	−35.1	71	37	33	29	17
Dunn, Wisconsin	−41.4	62	29	33	38	19

(continued on next page)

SUMMARY

Summary Table (continued)

	PERCENTAGE CHANGE IN PHYSICAL ASSET VALUE, 1930-1940	DISTRIBUTION OF PHYSICAL ASSET VALUE				DWELLINGS AS A PER CENT OF FARM REAL ESTATE VALUE, 1930
		Land & Buildings	Land	Buildings	Non-Real-Estate Assets	
Eastern Dairy Counties						
Trumbull, Ohio	−12.7%	76%	34%	42%	24%	29%
Chester, Pennsylvania	−15.7	77	30	47	22	28
Frederick, Maryland	−15.5	72	36	36	28	24
Hampden, Massachusetts	−17.4	80	33	47	19	30
Blair, Pennsylvania	−17.8	70	30	40	29	28
Orange, Vermont	−21.5	63	25	38	37	32
Livingston, New York	−27.5	68	31	37	32	25
Tioga, Pennsylvania	−29.5	61	24	37	39	28
Miscellaneous Counties						
Suwannee, Florida	−1.7	72	45	27	28	20
Blount, Tennessee	−1.9	81	53	28	19	17
Shelby, Kentucky	−6.6	82	53	29	18	20
Washington, Illinois	−10.9	78	53	25	22	17
Mason, Michigan	−11.0	72	33	39	28	28
Morrow, Ohio	−11.8	76	38	38	24	25
Independence, Arkansas	−13.6	73	51	22	27	19
Jefferson Davis, Louisiana	−13.8	76	63	13	24	11
Calvert, Maryland	−15.1	85	40	45	15	29
Prince Edward, Virginia	−22.3	80	44	36	20	31
Pike, Indiana	−25.2	77	53	24	23	20
Cumberland, New Jersey	−26.3	78	34	44	22	32
Kent, Delaware	−26.5	74	35	39	26	23
McCracken, Kentucky	−27.2	80	49	31	20	23
Wythe, Virginia	−27.4	84	59	25	16	16
Douglas, Oregon	−27.5	81	61	20	19	12
Berkeley, West Virginia	−34.0	81	44	37	19	19
Benton, Arkansas	−34.2	79	49	30	21	20

(continued on next page)

Summary Table (continued)

	Physical Assets per Farm (000)	Cropland as Per Cent of Total Acreage[a]	Off-Farm Work per Farm Operator, 1939 (in days)	Index of Rural Level of Living 1940[b]
Range Livestock Counties				
Tom Green, Texas	$22.3	13%	43	97
Catron, New Mexico	8.0	1	48	64
Webb, Texas	37.9	3	48	69
Carter, Oklahoma	4.1	35	40	89
Siskiyou, California	16.0	17	54	134
Yavapai, Arizona	15.1	1	56	106
Brewster, Texas	58.5	1	64	62
Chautauqua, Kansas	7.6	25	23	109
Elko, Nevada	38.5	2	33	109
San Miguel, New Mexico	5.7	4	52	28
Union, Oregon	12.4	31	67	125
Custer, Montana	13.5	6	35	108
Union, New Mexico	10.9	6	43	91
Dawes, Nebraska	13.1	3	27	124
Haakon, South Dakota	8.2	1	26	113
Corn Belt Counties				
Daviess, Kentucky	6.9	53	34	94
Wayne, Indiana	11.1	56	62	132
Putnam, Ohio	11.0	70	15	130
Douglas, Illinois	28.5	82	21	127
Calhoun, Michigan	6.7	39	62	137
Green, Wisconsin	14.6	49	13	130
Stark, Illinois	23.1	70	12	134
Hamilton, Iowa	22.6	75	14	137
Cherokee, Iowa	22.6	69	7	136
Appanoose, Iowa	6.8	38	38	97
Day, South Dakota	9.1	69	12	116
Cass, Missouri	8.1	52	33	111
Pierce, Nebraska	11.0	71	12	120
Franklin, Nebraska	7.8	56	19	111
Eastern Cotton Counties				
Jenkins, Georgia	5.8	47	11	67
Dillon, South Carolina	6.9	50	11	74
Edgecombe, North Carolina	14.0	45	13	75
Gordon, Georgia	3.9	32	21	84
Warren, Mississippi	3.0	17	37	56
Hardeman, Tennessee	3.3	26	23	72
Greene, Georgia	2.4	29	26	75
Wilcox, Georgia	4.9	42	15	73
Lee, Alabama	2.9	35	33	54
Kershaw, South Carolina	4.4	33	44	60
Tishomingo, Mississippi	1.5	28	35	74
Etowah, Alabama	3.6	28	48	77
Lowndes, Alabama	2.0	35	18	40
Coahoma, Mississippi	24.4	71	11	64
Lauderdale, Mississippi	2.7	29	32	69

(continued on next page)

Summary Table (continued)

	Physical Assets per Farm (000)	Cropland as Per Cent of Total Acreage[a]	Off-Farm Work per Farm Operator, 1939 (in days)	Index of Rural Level of Living 1940[b]
Western Cotton Counties				
Crittenden, Arkansas	$12.2	68%	15	64
Tyler, Texas	2.1	18	79	80
Chicot, Arkansas	4.7	48	14	63
Upshur, Texas	2.8	31	37	85
Natchitoches, Louisiana	3.5	42	20	53
Lubbock, Texas	13.4	72	25	127
St. Landry, Louisiana	3.5	63	13	43
Nolan, Texas	13.9	23	32	120
Cleveland, Oklahoma	5.9	36	30	94
Young, Texas	8.6	24	42	103
Bradley, Arkansas	2.3	35	32	72
Burleson, Texas	4.9	31	26	75
Washita, Oklahoma	8.5	60	23	111
Kaufman, Texas	7.0	50	24	89
DeWitt, Texas	6.7	26	32	82
Wheat Belt Counties				
Adams, Washington	39.1	72	16	147
Polk, Minnesota	10.0	70	15	116
Garfield, Oklahoma	15.2	66	32	126
Hill, Montana	10.4	40	39	106
Hansford, Texas	28.3	58	49	138
Rush, Kansas	15.4	73	23	119
Cheyenne, Nebraska	14.3	65	29	126
Williams, North Dakota	7.0	59	20	98
Day, South Dakota	9.1	68	12	116
Benson, North Dakota	4.4	70	20	104
Hettinger, North Dakota	9.5	62	18	109
Decatur, Kansas	9.0	56	27	115
Logan, Kansas	9.3	43	40	119
Franklin, Nebraska	7.8	56	19	111
Hyde, South Dakota	7.2	41	15	120
Western Dairy Counties				
Koochiching, Minnesota	3.7	20	78	85
Alpena, Michigan	4.9	33	49	96
Sanilac, Michigan	6.9	59	24	127
Shiawassee, Michigan	8.1	60	39	127
Polk, Minnesota	10.0	70	15	116
Winnebago, Wisconsin	12.7	60	26	123
Calhoun, Michigan	6.7	50	60	137
Green, Wisconsin	14.6	49	13	130
Wood, Wisconsin	7.7	39	43	121
Meeker, Minnesota	11.7	67	11	125
Ashland, Wisconsin	3.7	27	52	101
Winona, Minnesota	11.9	47	15	125
Dunn, Wisconsin	7.8	45	19	118

(continued on next page)

Summary Table (continued)

	Physical Assets per Farm (000)	Cropland as Per Cent of Total Acreage[a]	Off-Farm Work per Farm Operator, 1939 (in days)	Index of Rural Level of Living 1940[b]
Eastern Dairy Counties				
Trumbull, Ohio	$5.7	41%	86	125
Chester, Pennsylvania	17.2	55	49	137
Frederick, Maryland	9.0	58	42	111
Hampden, Massachusetts	7.0	24	99	141
Blair, Pennsylvania	6.0	51	83	115
Orange, Vermont	5.3	24	66	126
Livingston, New York	10.1	51	44	136
Tioga, Pennsylvania	5.8	39	50	124
Miscellaneous Counties				
Suwannee, Florida	2.9	32	19	68
Blount, Tennessee	4.6	34	97	89
Shelby, Kentucky	12.5	30	23	113
Washington, Illinois	8.1	61	17	100
Mason, Michigan	5.3	39	36	113
Morrow, Ohio	6.3	46	30	120
Independence, Arkansas	2.3	29	60	73
Jefferson Davis, Louisiana	9.7	38	29	65
Calvert, Maryland	6.3	19	29	92
Prince Edward, Virginia	3.0	19	45	74
Pike, Indiana	3.9	39	62	98
Cumberland, New Jersey	6.8	51	55	125
Kent, Delaware	6.4	43	34	112
McCracken, Kentucky	3.4	38	62	93
Wythe, Virginia	8.5	22	72	86
Douglas, Oregon	7.8	12	60	116
Berkeley, West Virginia	7.3	42	59	101
Benton, Arkansas	3.0	26	38	91

(continued on next page)

Summary Table (continued)

	Live-stock	Crops	Dairy Products	Poul-try[c]	Used by Farm Household	FARM PRODUCT VALUE, 1939 (PER $1,000 OF TOTAL PHYSICAL ASSETS)
	DISTRIBUTION OF FARM PRODUCT VALUE, 1939					
Range Livestock Counties						
Tom Green, Texas	63%	16%	9%	3%	9%	$103
Catron, New Mexico	79	3	1	1	16	179
Webb, Texas	59	35	4	–	2	130
Carter, Oklahoma	27	26	11	6	30	171
Siskiyou, California	31	38	19	3	9	182
Yavapai, Arizona	71	6	10	4	10	156
Brewster, Texas	91	1	2	–	6	113
Chautauqua, Kansas	53	18	9	5	15	169
Elko, Nevada	87	7	1	–	5	150
San Miguel, New Mexico	69	7	7	1	16	138
Union, Oregon	40	32	14	2	12	151
Custer, Montana	57	27	7	2	7	162
Union, New Mexico	82	4	4	2	8	161
Dawes, Nebraska	65	17	6	3	9	145
Haakon, South Dakota	70	13	4	4	9	127
Corn Belt Counties						
Daviess, Kentucky	20	48	8	6	18	154
Wayne, Indiana	41	31	13	6	9	180
Putnam, Ohio	30	37	10	13	10	162
Douglas, Illinois	17	70	4	3	6	123
Calhoun, Michigan	27	23	25	9	16	168
Green, Wisconsin	33	3	50	5	9	164
Stark, Illinois	37	50	5	3	5	145
Hamilton, Iowa	40	42	6	6	6	156
Cherokee, Iowa	57	31	4	3	5	205
Appanoose, Iowa	45	15	10	11	19	150
Day, South Dakota	23	44	13	8	12	177
Cass, Missouri	33	25	16	11	15	156
Pierce, Nebraska	51	19	9	8	13	131
Franklin, Nebraska	34	32	10	11	13	125

(continued on next page)

Summary Table (*continued*)

	DISTRIBUTION OF FARM PRODUCT VALUE, 1939					FARM PRODUCT VALUE, 1939 (PER $1,000 OF TOTAL PHYSICAL ASSETS)
	Live-stock	Crops	Dairy Products	Poul-try[c]	Used by Farm Household	
Eastern Cotton Counties						
Jenkins, Georgia	8%	67%	1%	2%	22%	$291
Dillon, South Carolina	2	83	1	1	13	288
Edgecombe, North Carolina	4	83	1	1	11	317
Gordon, Georgia	2	59	5	4	30	222
Warren, Mississippi	12	43	7	4	34	202
Hardeman, Tennessee	9	47	5	2	37	242
Greene, Georgia	4	44	6	2	44	261
Wilcox, Georgia	5	70	1	1	23	277
Lee, Alabama	6	50	14	3	27	251
Kershaw, South Carolina	5	69	2	2	22	278
Tishomingo, Mississippi	6	32	2	4	56	264
Etowah, Alabama	3	52	7	3	35	204
Lowndes, Alabama	18	46	7	2	27	238
Coahoma, Mississippi	1	88	1	–	10	230
Lauderdale, Mississippi	9	31	15	2	43	214
Western Cotton Counties						
Crittenden, Arkansas	3	84	–	–	13	285
Tyler, Texas	13	19	3	5	60	217
Chicot, Arkansas	2	77	1	1	19	257
Upshur, Texas	8	41	10	3	38	226
Natchitoches, Louisiana	4	64	3	1	28	243
Lubbock, Texas	13	64	11	4	8	169
St. Landry, Louisiana	4	66	1	3	26	252
Nolan, Texas	47	36	5	5	7	139
Cleveland, Oklahoma	18	37	16	7	22	146
Young, Texas	52	16	8	6	18	111
Bradley, Arkansas	9	52	3	2	34	295
Burleson, Texas	12	60	2	7	19	200
Washita, Oklahoma	13	57	11	4	15	160
Kaufman, Texas	10	68	4	3	15	185
DeWitt, Texas	34	22	7	21	16	146

(continued on next page)

Summary Table (continued)

	Livestock	Crops	Dairy Products	Poultry[c]	Used by Farm Household	FARM PRODUCT VALUE, 1939 (PER $1,000 OF TOTAL PHYSICAL ASSETS)
	DISTRIBUTION OF FARM PRODUCT VALUE, 1939					
Wheat Belt Counties						
Adams, Washington	7%	86%	1%	3%	3%	$156
Polk, Minnesota	15	50	17	7	11	176
Garfield, Oklahoma	13	67	8	5	7	141
Hill, Montana	14	71	4	4	7	170
Hansford, Texas	71	26	1	1	1	341
Rush, Kansas	39	19	11	11	20	54
Cheyenne, Nebraska	21	64	5	5	5	153
Williams, North Dakota	10	58	12	5	15	111
Day, South Dakota	23	44	13	8	12	177
Benson, North Dakota	14	62	10	4	10	217
Hettinger, North Dakota	9	66	8	4	13	154
Decatur, Kansas	47	18	10	9	16	89
Logan, Kansas	50	27	8	5	10	104
Franklin, Nebraska	34	32	10	11	13	125
Hyde, South Dakota	47	24	8	10	11	159
Western Dairy Counties						
Koochiching, Minnesota	12	30	22	8	28	149
Alpena, Michigan	17	29	21	7	26	171
Sanilac, Michigan	15	38	28	7	12	218
Shiawassee, Michigan	18	35	25	11	11	159
Polk, Minnesota	15	50	16	8	11	176
Winnebago, Wisconsin	19	13	50	7	11	134
Calhoun, Michigan	27	23	25	9	16	168
Green, Wisconsin	33	3	50	5	9	164
Wood, Wisconsin	14	15	52	5	14	156
Meeker, Minnesota	26	29	24	10	11	178
Ashland, Wisconsin	10	10	47	4	29	188
Winona, Minnesota	29	16	30	10	15	147
Dunn, Wisconsin	21	7	49	6	17	177

(continued on next page)

Summary Table (continued)

	Live-stock	Crops	Dairy Products	Poul-try[c]	Used by Farm Household	FARM PRODUCT VALUE, 1939 (PER $1,000 OF TOTAL PHYSICAL ASSETS)
			DISTRIBUTION OF FARM PRODUCT VALUE, 1939			
Eastern Dairy Counties						
Trumbull, Ohio	10%	23%	37%	11%	19%	$155
Chester, Pennsylvania	8	36	39	10	7	175
Frederick, Maryland	12	23	44	8	13	213
Hampden, Massachusetts	5	35	29	18	13	221
Blair, Pennsylvania	6	37	29	11	17	219
Orange, Vermont	12	15	48	8	16	259
Livingston, New York	14	37	33	6	10	210
Tioga, Pennsylvania	12	8	56	11	13	226
Miscellaneous Counties						
Suwannee, Florida	14	55	2	3	26	265
Blount, Tennessee	21	17	15	6	41	122
Shelby, Kentucky	20	48	20	2	10	169
Washington, Illinois	9	45	19	11	16	176
Mason, Michigan	16	28	31	6	19	167
Morrow, Ohio	38	13	18	11	19	160
Independence, Arkansas	10	37	5	4	44	280
Jefferson Davis, Louisiana	6	83	2	–	9	253
Calvert, Maryland	3	79	–	3	15	227
Prince Edward, Virginia	6	46	12	5	31	204
Pike, Indiana	36	27	6	11	20	169
Cumberland, New Jersey	1	49	8	36	6	368
Kent, Delaware	7	39	20	20	14	213
McCracken, Kentucky	15	34	16	5	30	187
Wythe, Virginia	39	18	8	6	29	125
Douglas, Oregon	28	20	10	26	16	163
Berkeley, West Virginia	11	50	11	8	20	209
Benton, Arkansas	15	16	12	35	22	231

(continued on next page)

161

Summary Table (continued)

	INTEREST IN PHYSICAL ASSETS OF:			PER CENT OF ALL FARMS WITH PART OF REAL ESTATE EQUITY HELD BY:			MTG. DEBT AS % OF VALUE OF MTGD. FARMS
	Operators	Landlords	Creditors	Operators	Landlords	Creditors	
Range Livestock Counties							
Tom Green, Texas	42.2%	38.1%	19.6%	58%	51%	51%	25%
Catron, New Mexico	52.4	29.3	18.2	85	34	16	22
Webb, Texas	40.7	46.1	13.2	59	49	27	14
Carter, Oklahoma	52.9	28.6	18.4	43	68	33	33
Siskiyou, California	55.3	22.2	22.5	76	39	42	35
Yavapai, Arizona	51.5	27.9	20.5	78	43	34	38
Brewster, Texas	41.4	42.3	16.3	50	63	53	23
Chautauqua, Kansas	43.2	31.6	25.2	53	64	35	45
Elko, Nevada	46.1	34.7	19.1	88	18	31	44
San Miguel, New Mexico	35.7	43.1	21.2	88	24	17	37
Union, Oregon	55.5	20.7	23.7	81	36	55	42
Custer, Montana	39.1	35.3	25.6	66	68	27	46
Union, New Mexico	36.0	39.8	24.1	64	73	58	42
Dawes, Nebraska	40.5	27.9	31.5	54	71	52	46
Haakon, South Dakota	35.7	27.6	36.7	76	80	45	50
Corn Belt Counties							
Daviess, Kentucky	54.0	28.9	17.1	55	52	41	37
Wayne, Indiana	53.2	28.0	18.8	67	41	51	37
Putnam, Ohio	50.4	28.5	21.1	64	52	49	37
Douglas, Illinois	30.8	50.6	18.6	45	75	45	38
Calhoun, Michigan	61.8	18.2	20.0	67	41	51	45
Green, Wisconsin	47.3	26.1	26.6	57	47	51	62
Stark, Illinois	34.5	42.1	23.4	47	66	48	41
Hamilton, Iowa	33.9	33.6	32.5	50	61	57	50
Cherokee, Iowa	33.8	38.2	28.0	40	70	54	49
Appanoose, Iowa	58.2	23.1	18.7	65	47	38	46
Day, South Dakota	35.0	31.0	34.0	49	72	48	52
Cass, Missouri	39.9	34.8	25.3	53	61	47	48
Pierce, Nebraska	33.3	36.2	30.5	37	74	47	50
Franklin, Nebraska	36.7	32.8	30.5	49	52	50	59

(continued on next page)

162

Summary Table (continued)

	INTEREST IN PHYSICAL ASSETS OF:			PER CENT OF ALL FARMS WITH PART OF REAL ESTATE EQUITY HELD BY:			MTG. DEBT AS % OF VALUE OF MTGD. FARMS
	Operators	Landlords	Creditors	Operators	Landlords	Creditors	
Eastern Cotton Counties							
Jenkins, Georgia	44.2%	30.3%	25.5%	58%	49%	51%	36%
Dillon, South Carolina	28.4	55.1	16.5	38	66	48	26
Edgecombe, North Carolina	18.9	61.8	19.3	57	52	44	37
Gordon, Georgia	47.4	36.9	15.7	53	50	37	37
Warren, Mississippi	53.6	24.4	22.0	44	61	26	35
Hardeman, Tennessee	40.0	40.5	19.5	50	55	37	38
Greene, Georgia	46.0	19.9	34.1	37	70	33	35
Wilcox, Georgia	33.1	34.9	32.0	54	53	47	41
Lee, Alabama	39.7	25.6	34.7	40	65	39	38
Kershaw, South Carolina	41.7	34.1	24.2	55	52	37	32
Tishomingo, Mississippi	53.2	22.2	24.6	58	49	38	34
Etowah, Alabama	48.1	26.9	25.0	56	50	46	36
Lowndes, Alabama	43.6	25.4	31.0	20	87	51	37
Coahoma, Mississippi	15.3	54.4	30.3	41	65	65	37
Lauderdale, Mississippi	49.4	25.5	25.1	71	34	35	33
Western Cotton Counties							
Crittenden, Arkansas	43.1	19.6	37.3	32	72	54	29
Tyler, Texas	72.4	7.8	19.8	72	33	13	24
Chicot, Arkansas	33.4	26.6	40.0	43	61	44	33
Upshur, Texas	60.2	17.5	22.3	60	51	21	30
Natchitoches, Louisiana	43.5	24.9	31.6	54	53	39	40
Lubbock, Texas	36.6	28.1	35.3	53	58	63	39
St. Landry, Louisiana	35.4	14.5	50.1	33	70	39	37
Nolan, Texas	38.5	27.1	34.4	55	59	39	31
Cleveland, Oklahoma	47.2	18.5	34.3	49	61	65	30
Young, Texas	47.4	21.6	31.0	60	57	41	32
Bradley, Arkansas	54.5	31.1	14.4	69	39	27	38
Burleson, Texas	52.2	17.1	30.7	54	60	47	36
Washita, Oklahoma	44.4	24.6	31.0	53	61	29	38
Kaufman, Texas	28.6	23.9	47.5	44	67	60	43
DeWitt, Texas	56.8	14.9	28.3	57	53	37	43

(continued on next page)

Summary Table (continued)

	INTEREST IN PHYSICAL ASSETS OF:			PER CENT OF ALL FARMS WITH PART OF REAL ESTATE EQUITY HELD BY:			MTG. DEBT AS % OF VALUE OF MTGD. FARMS
	Operators	Landlords	Creditors	Operators	Landlords	Creditors	
Wheat Belt Counties							
Adams, Washington	45.9%	38.8%	15.3%	60%	76%	47%	28%
Polk, Minnesota	52.9	25.9	21.2	70	52	52	43
Garfield, Oklahoma	47.4	35.7	16.9	55	64	44	30
Hill, Montana	43.6	28.9	27.5	75	74	49	36
Hansford, Texas	32.7	37.1	31.2	60	72	64	44
Rush, Kansas	38.6	39.2	22.2	54	76	54	38
Cheyenne, Nebraska	38.2	39.3	22.5	48	83	51	40
Williams, North Dakota	20.8	28.9	50.3	61	71	49	64
Day, South Dakota	33.7	32.6	33.7	49	78	48	52
Benson, North Dakota	32.2	31.5	36.3	50	77	46	63
Hettinger, North Dakota	26.4	33.5	40.1	57	82	49	63
Decatur, Kansas	27.3	35.4	37.3	54	71	51	49
Logan, Kansas	23.1	33.9	43.0	62	72	52	59
Franklin, Nebraska	36.7	32.8	30.5	49	52	50	59
Hyde, South Dakota	32.4	31.2	36.4	37	93	28	57
Western Dairy Counties							
Koochiching, Minnesota	76.4	5.6	18.0	93	13	44	32
Alpena, Michigan	83.3	4.7	12.0	92	13	38	33
Sanilac, Michigan	71.5	11.2	17.2	81	33	47	44
Shiawassee, Michigan	65.2	16.7	18.1	77	38	50	42
Polk, Minnesota	55.3	23.5	21.2	70	52	52	43
Winnebago, Wisconsin	65.6	12.9	21.4	79	30	55	48
Calhoun, Michigan	64.2	15.8	19.9	77	32	52	45
Green, Wisconsin	53.0	20.4	26.6	57	47	51	62
Wood, Wisconsin	63.1	12.5	24.4	81	34	52	56
Meeker, Minnesota	51.4	21.3	27.3	63	51	54	53
Ashland, Wisconsin	76.3	5.4	18.2	90	17	45	49
Winona, Minnesota	58.2	17.4	24.3	68	41	48	47
Dunn, Wisconsin	62.8	12.9	24.3	74	38	50	59

(continued on next page)

164

Summary Table (continued)

	INTEREST IN PHYSICAL ASSETS OF:			PER CENT OF ALL FARMS WITH PART OF REAL ESTATE EQUITY HELD BY:			MTG. DEBT AS % OF VALUE OF MTGD. FARMS
	Operators	Landlords	Creditors	Operators	Landlords	Creditors	
Eastern Dairy Counties							
Trumbull, Ohio	72.4%	10.3%	17.2%	86%	20%	42%	42%
Chester, Pennsylvania	63.6	20.4	16.0	79	27	48	35
Frederick, Maryland	69.5	15.1	15.4	71	30	33	50
Hampden, Massachusetts	68.9	10.1	21.0	92	12	58	36
Blair, Pennsylvania	68.7	14.5	16.8	80	22	35	43
Orange, Vermont	76.2	5.1	18.7	91	16	46	42
Livingston, New York	60.3	19.1	20.6	77	40	47	44
Tioga, Pennsylvania	68.1	10.2	21.7	83	26	40	47
Miscellaneous Counties							
Suwannee, Florida	54.5	20.5	25.0	78	35	41	32
Blount, Tennessee	74.3	15.5	10.2	87	21	28	37
Shelby, Kentucky	55.4	26.8	17.8	67	37	46	36
Washington, Illinois	55.8	35.6	8.6	57	64	17	39
Mason, Michigan	66.6	8.9	24.4	86	26	54	39
Morrow, Ohio	58.8	24.6	16.5	69	39	41	42
Independence, Arkansas	53.2	30.4	16.4	61	52	33	31
Jefferson Davis, Louisiana	23.5	51.9	24.6	46	69	40	44
Calvert, Maryland	47.7	39.2	13.1	64	39	34	23
Prince Edward, Virginia	66.4	18.5	15.1	80	31	25	33
Pike, Indiana	59.6	21.3	19.1	79	45	41	34
Cumberland, New Jersey	57.8	15.7	26.5	90	19	51	46
Kent, Delaware	51.3	32.3	16.4	61	42	39	41
McCracken, Kentucky	65.5	19.9	14.6	78	37	28	37
Wythe, Virginia	71.7	18.0	10.3	80	24	22	31
Douglas, Oregon	69.5	14.3	16.2	81	29	45	34
Berkeley, West Virginia	57.0	23.5	19.5	75	32	32	43
Benton, Arkansas	60.1	22.4	17.5	69	39	36	39

(continued on next page)

Summary Table (continued)

	FARM MTG. HOLDINGS, AS % OF TOTAL FARM REAL ESTATE VALUE, OF:				NON-REAL-ESTATE LOANS, AS % OF TOTAL NON-REAL-ESTATE FARM ASSETS, OF:	
	FLB's & FFMC	Ins. & Mtg. Inv. Cos.	Coml. & Savings Banks	Indiv. & Misc.	Banks and PCA's	FSA and ECFL Division of FCA
Range Livestock Counties						
Tom Green, Texas	8%	–	–	6%	45%	2%
Catron, New Mexico	–	–	3%	7	16	3
Webb, Texas	3	–	–	8	8	–
Carter, Oklahoma	2	4%	–	6	10	10
Siskiyou, California	12	1	1	6	15	1
Yavapai, Arizona	2	–	2	11	16	2
Brewster, Texas	8	–	–	6	8	3
Chautauqua, Kansas	8	3	2	5	26	5
Elko, Nevada	10	–	–	11	2	1
San Miguel, New Mexico	5	2	–	9	8	10
Union, Oregon	13	4	–	7	5	4
Custer, Montana	6	2	1	9	16	11
Union, New Mexico	15	2	–	1	7	16
Dawes, Nebraska	16	3	1	5	26	10
Haakon, South Dakota	8	–	1	14	24	24
Corn Belt Counties						
Daviess, Kentucky	10	3	1	2	8	2
Wayne, Indiana	9	4	2	3	11	1
Putnam, Ohio	7	7	3	3	15	1
Douglas, Illinois	7	8	–	2	15	1
Calhoun, Michigan	9	4	2	3	6	3
Green, Wisconsin	9	1	4	20	6	1
Stark, Illinois	10	8	1	–	24	2
Hamilton, Iowa	10	13	2	5	26	1
Cherokee, Iowa	8	11	3	3	20	1
Appanoose, Iowa	8	3	3	7	7	2
Day, South Dakota	19	2	–	5	8	21
Cass, Missouri	7	8	3	6	14	3
Pierce, Nebraska	15	10	1	7	10	4
Franklin, Nebraska	11	6	1	11	10	17

(continued on next page)

Summary Table (continued)

	FLB's & FFMC	Ins. & Mtg. Inv. Cos.	Coml. & Savings Banks	Indiv. & Misc.	Banks and PCA's	FSA and ECFL Division of FCA
	FARM MTG. HOLDINGS, AS % OF TOTAL FARM REAL ESTATE VALUE, OF:				NON-REAL-ESTATE LOANS, AS % OF TOTAL NON-REAL-ESTATE FARM ASSETS, OF:	
astern Cotton Counties						
Jenkins, Georgia	10%	1%	3%	4%	16%	15%
Dillon, South Carolina	5	3	–	6	13	4
Edgecombe, North Carolina	6	4	2	5	17	2
Gordon, Georgia	11	–	1	4	1	7
Warren, Mississippi	6	–	8	1	21	6
Hardeman, Tennessee	9	1	4	3	13	3
Greene, Georgia	7	–	2	5	12	55
Wilcox, Georgia	10	8	2	2	24	14
Lee, Alabama	8	–	4	5	46	9
Kershaw, South Carolina	12	–	1	5	13	15
Tishomingo, Mississippi	9	–	1	5	10	20
Etowah, Alabama	10	2	2	4	13	16
Lowndes, Alabama	10	1	2	7	22	11
Coahoma, Mississippi	6	14	1	7	25	1
Lauderdale, Mississippi	11	1	1	3	20	14
estern Cotton Counties						
Crittenden, Arkansas	4	10	2	4	7	2
Tyler, Texas	2	–	2	1	5	6
Chicot, Arkansas	4	6	2	8	21	10
Upshur, Texas	6	–	1	2	10	20
Natchitoches, Louisiana	10	2	2	1	22	10
Lubbock, Texas	16	4	–	2	29	5
St. Landry, Louisiana	10	4	1	3	4	2
Nolan, Texas	14	5	1	1	23	8
Cleveland, Oklahoma	4	2	1	8	15	4
Young, Texas	8	1	1	4	30	4
Bradley, Arkansas	8	1	3	4	25	18
Burleson, Texas	9	–	–	6	16	3
Washita, Oklahoma	7	8	–	9	14	3
Kaufman, Texas	7	9	1	2	21	7
DeWitt, Texas	7	1	–	5	11	1

(continued on next page)

Summary Table (continued)

	FARM MTG. HOLDINGS, AS % OF TOTAL FARM REAL ESTATE VALUE, OF:				NON-REAL-ESTATE LOANS, AS % OF TOTAL NON-REAL-ESTATE FARM ASSETS, OF:	
	FLB's & FFMC	Ins. & Mtg. Inv. Cos.	Coml. & Savings Banks	Indiv. & Misc.	Banks and PCA's	FSA and ECF Division of FCA
Wheat Belt Counties						
Adams, Washington	8%	3%	–	3%	9%	4%
Polk, Minnesota	8	2	1%	6	8	2
Garfield, Oklahoma	5	6	2	3	11	2
Hill, Montana	8	1	–	6	9	23
Hansford, Texas	22	–	2	4	15	17
Rush, Kansas	11	7	1	3	14	6
Cheyenne, Nebraska	16	3	–	1	9	7
Williams, North Dakota	22	–	–	2	7	74
Day, South Dakota	19	1	–	5	8	21
Benson, North Dakota	20	1	–	4	6	23
Hettinger, North Dakota	21	–	1	6	9	30
Decatur, Kansas	19	1	2	5	29	30
Logan, Kansas	19	–	1	4	31	31
Franklin, Nebraska	11	6	1	11	10	17
Hyde, South Dakota	9	–	–	7	9	30
Western Dairy Counties						
Koochiching, Minnesota	6	–	1	5	8	5
Alpena, Michigan	9	–	2	3	3	2
Sanilac, Michigan	10	1	1	9	6	1
Shiawassee, Michigan	8	1	2	8	7	1
Polk, Minnesota	8	2	1	6	8	2
Winnebago, Wisconsin	6	2	1	15	4	–
Calhoun, Michigan	10	2	3	8	6	3
Green, Wisconsin	9	1	4	20	6	–
Wood, Wisconsin	13	1	2	12	6	1
Meeker, Minnesota	14	3	2	9	9	3
Ashland, Wisconsin	11	1	3	4	2	3
Winona, Minnesota	13	1	2	8	9	1
Dunn, Wisconsin	13	2	4	12	6	3

(concluded on next page)

Summary Table (concluded)

	FARM MTG. HOLDINGS, AS % OF TOTAL FARM REAL ESTATE VALUE, OF:				NON-REAL-ESTATE LOANS, AS % OF TOTAL NON-REAL-ESTATE FARM ASSETS, OF:	
	FLB's & FFMC	Ins. & Mtg. Inv. Cos.	Coml. & Savings Banks	Indiv. & Misc.	Banks and PCA's	FSA and ECFL Division of FCA
Eastern Dairy Counties						
Trumbull, Ohio	5%	—	2%	10%	7%	1%
Chester, Pennsylvania	1	1%	5	7	8	—
Frederick, Maryland	2	—	5	9	5	1
Hampden, Massachusetts	6	—	3	12	6	1
Blair, Pennsylvania	5	—	3	9	6	1
Orange, Vermont	5	—	2	10	6	3
Livingston, New York	6	—	5	7	9	1
Tioga, Pennsylvania	3	1	6	11	11	2
Miscellaneous Counties						
Suwannee, Florida	8	—	3	2	20	14
Blount, Tennessee	2	3	1	5	3	—
Shelby, Kentucky	13	2	2	2	8	—
Washington, Illinois	1	—	1	5	8	—
Mason, Michigan	11	—	2	9	17	2
Morrow, Ohio	7	3	2	6	5	3
Independence, Arkansas	4	—	1	6	8	10
Jefferson Davis, Louisiana	14	3	2	3	18	2
Calvert, Maryland	2	—	3	6	11	4
Prince Edward, Virginia	6	1	1	3	12	8
Pike, Indiana	6	1	5	3	18	2
Cumberland, New Jersey	5	2	2	17	14	3
Kent, Delaware	3	—	8	6	6	3
McCracken, Kentucky	7	1	1	5	6	2
Wythe, Virginia	7	—	2	1	4	3
Douglas, Oregon	7	1	1	8	9	1
Berkeley, West Virginia	6	1	5	2	27	4
Benton, Arkansas	6	2	1	6	9	8

Footnotes to Summary Table

a Cropland excludes plowable pasture.
b M. J. Hagood, *Rural Level of Living Indexes for Counties of the United States, 1940*, Department of Agriculture, 1943.
c Includes poultry and other livestock products.

APPENDIX A

SOURCES OF DATA AND METHODS OF ESTIMATING
INDICATORS OF THE ECONOMIC AND FINANCIAL
CHARACTERISTICS OF AGRICULTURE

THIS appendix reviews briefly the sources from which the basic data were drawn and indicates, in as detailed a manner as space allows, the procedures that were followed in adapting them for use in the study. In most instances these adaptations were extensive. For this reason it would be well for the reader to regard the results as merely estimates descriptive of the characteristics of agriculture, and to bear in mind that they should be employed in other connections only with a full appreciation of their unavoidable shortcomings.

Indicators of Asset and Product Characteristics

TOTAL PHYSICAL ASSETS

For each county the reported value of land, buildings, livestock, and implements and machinery was taken directly from the 1940 Census of Agriculture; to this were added estimates of crops, feed, fertilizer, and other miscellaneous supplies on hand at the beginning of the year. Estimates for the latter items were derived from a number of sources, principally agricultural experiment station bulletins reporting local studies based on farm records. Since the data are for the beginning of the year, the actual value of growing crops was excluded except in areas where such crops were likely to be maturing at that time. No comprehensive body of data on which to base these estimates of the value of growing crops was available; we therefore made allowance for them by increasing moderately the percentage of total assets represented by non-real-estate assets in those counties where this item was thought to be significant. In general, the amount of non-real-estate assets other than livetstock and implements and machinery is so small relative to total assets that even a fairly large error in estimating crop value would result in only a moderate error in the estimate of total physical assets.

Household equipment and other personal effects of the farm family were excluded from total physical assets, although from many viewpoints they may properly be regarded as assets of the

170

combined firm–farm home. The omission of these categories for which data are unavailable causes an understatement of the total, but this is not serious where, as in this study, measures based on total asset size of farm are employed only to indicate intercounty differences.

AVERAGE PHYSICAL ASSETS PER FARM

The average of physical assets per farm for each county is affected, of course, by the estimates of both total physical assets and number of farms, the latter being considered identical with the number of farm operators, exclusive of croppers. The exclusion of croppers helps to make the average farm size of the southern counties comparable to the averages for other areas, but it is at best a rough adjustment and the results must be interpreted with this fact in mind. However, since the sample was chosen to show extremes in kinds of agriculture, the per farm data serve reasonably well to indicate intercounty differences in average assets per farm even where they do not accurately measure *the amount* of this difference.

COMPOSITION OF PHYSICAL ASSETS

While the division of real estate value between land and buildings is somewhat artificial as a measure of asset composition for a particular farm, it is usable as a means of comparing all farms in one county with those in another. For example, the farms in counties in which census figures show land to equal 75 per cent of the value of all real estate assets are clearly different from the farms in counties in which land is shown to be only 50 per cent of such assets.

In computations of *the percentage of total acreage in cropland*, cropland acreage includes cropland harvested, acreage in land involving crop failure, and idle or fallow cropland. Plowable pasture is excluded. The *value of farmers' dwellings* is taken directly from the 1930 Census of Agriculture.

PRODUCT CHARACTERISTICS OF FARMS

Data on the distribution of the value of farm product sales by type of product were taken directly from the 1940 Census of Agriculture, with sales of crops and livestock combined, since crops are frequently marketed via sales of livestock. For most purposes, the relative importance of crops, as compared with livestock raised on pasture, can be better evaluated by reference to the percentage of acreage in cropland than by direct comparisons of the respective product sales. Dairy product sales are self-explanatory. The third category includes sales of poultry and poultry products as well as a wide range of miscellaneous products. *Value of products consumed by the farm household* provides an indirect clue to the extent to which commercial farming is practiced; and *off-farm work per farm operator* is useful as a measure of the extent to which nonfarm occupations are combined with the operation of the farm.

The data on product composition are deficient in that they exclude certain products of the farm firm, such as housing, but intercounty differences in the importance of this service can be inferred from the ratio of the value of the farmers' dwellings to the value of total real estate. Likewise, the income derived from off-farm work is, in a sense, income derived from the farm, but differences in its importance among farms can only be inferred from the number of days of off-farm work performed yearly per farm operator. Although these two items cannot be included directly in the percentage distribution of farm product value, measures of them can be used to supplement the product data and thus to give a reasonably complete coverage of farm product throw-off.

Indicators of Financial Characteristics

Data on the financial characteristics of farms are less plentiful than data on the asset and product characteristics reviewed above, and those available are deficient in many respects. The basic objective is to indicate differences among counties in the capital structure of agriculture, but since most farms are organized on an individual proprietorship basis, a description of capital structure comparable to that available for corporate business is not feasible.

OPERATOR INTEREST IN TOTAL
PHYSICAL ASSETS

The dollar value of this interest includes the interest of both owner operators and tenants; in order to measure the extent to which agriculture draws its capital from active farmers, it also includes the equity interest that farm operators may have in farms other than those they operate. However, operator interest excludes whatever creditor interest operators may have in other farms, since we had no way of estimating this amount.

Separate estimates have been made of the interests of operators in real estate assets and non-real-estate assets. Census data provide a basis for estimating the interest of operators in farm real estate, and survey data obtained by the Department of Agriculture in a mailed questionnaire make it possible to estimate the value of the operator's equity interest in farm real estate other than that of the farm he operates.

Estimates of operator interest in non-real-estate assets were made as follows: From an estimate of total value of non-real-estate assets were deducted the reported non-real-estate loans of banks, Production Credit Associations, the Farm Security Administration, and the Emergency Crop and Feed Loan Division of the Farm Credit Administration, and an additional amount estimated to represent obligations to other sources of non-real-estate credit. In most counties this additional amount was estimated at about 40 per cent of total non-real-estate debt.

The estimate was then reduced to take account of the probable landlord interest in non-real-estate assets by shifting to landlords the entire equity in non-real-estate assets for cropper farms and a partial equity in the case of farms operated by share tenants. This procedure is far from precise, but it does take account of those situations in which the landlord interest in non-real-estate assets is relatively high. Moreover, it gives a measure which, when combined with the measure of operator interest in real estate, produces a reasonably accurate indicator of intercounty differences in operator interest in total physical assets.

The principal deficiency to be noted in this estimate is the adjustment that was necessary to take account of the non-real-estate loans made by individuals and miscellaneous lenders. The estimate is used, therefore, only in combination with the estimate of operator interest in real estate assets, which reduces appreciably the possible percentage error. Furthermore, the selection of extreme counties for the 108-county sample gives reasonable assurance that the indicated differences among counties with respect to operator interests in non-real-estate assets are real, even though the precise extent of the differences may not be represented reliably.

CREDITOR INTEREST IN PHYSICAL ASSETS

The measure of creditor interest in physical assets is based on three sources: estimates of total mortgage debt for owner-operated farms, constructed from the 1940 Census of Agricul-

173

ture; survey data for tenant- and manager-operated farms obtained from a mailed inquiry sent to farm owners; and the estimate of total non-real-estate debt used in obtaining a measure of operator interest in physical assets. As pointed out earlier, credit interests of farm operators and landlords are included in the category of creditor interest rather than in that of operator or landlord interest. Since debt relates to a somewhat larger universe than assets, the percentage creditor interest is overstated, but this is not serious insofar as the measures are used only to indicate intercounty differences.

LANDLORD INTEREST IN PHYSICAL ASSETS

Estimates of landlord interest are residuals, after deduction from total assets of the estimated interests of farm operators and creditors. The two major items in this computation are the value of farm real estate in tenant- and manager-operated farms and the estimated mortgage debt on these farms; the estimated landlord interest in non-real-estate assets is but a small percentage of the total landlord interest in most counties.

PERCENTAGE OF FARMS UNDER MORTGAGE

County estimates of the total number of mortgaged farms of full-owner and part-owner operators were made on the basis of data from the 1940 Census of Agriculture. The number of mortgaged farms operated by tenants and managers, on the other hand, was estimated from Department of Agriculture survey data. For the estimate of the number of mortgaged tenant- and manager-operated farms, cropper farms were deducted from tenant-operated farms before the survey data on the percentages of farms under mortgage were applied. The total number of farms, excluding cropper farms, was used also as the basis for the estimate of the percentage of all farms under mortgage. The resulting percentages are somewhat higher than would be obtained if cropper farms were included, but this fact probably improves their quality for purposes of comparison among counties.

RATIO OF MORTGAGE DEBT TO THE
VALUE OF MORTGAGED FARMS

Total farm mortgage debt was estimated in the manner described above, and the value of mortgaged full-owner and part-owner farms was derived from 1940 census data. Two bases were used to approximate the value of mortgaged farms operated by tenants and managers, namely the 1940 survey data and the relationship between the average values per farm of mortgaged and debt-free farms of full-owner operators. The estimate obtained on the latter basis was checked against independent estimates based on the 1940 survey data, and where substantial differences were found the data were further analyzed to produce a final estimate.

PERCENTAGE OF FARM MORTGAGE DEBT
HELD BY PRINCIPAL LENDER GROUPS

Estimated total farm mortgage debt by counties is the starting point for apportioning farm loans among the several lenders. Survey data and complete tabulations are available for federal land banks, the Federal Farm Mortgage Corporation, and commercial banks. County data for the first two are based on the original amount of loans outstanding in 1940; independent estimates were prepared on the basis of survey questionnaire data for groups of counties falling in major type-of-farming regions. County estimates based on original loan amount were then adjusted downward to bring them into line with the county group estimates based on *unpaid balance* data.

There is probably some upward bias in the loan estimates, since the responses to mailed questionnaires from farm owners whose mortgages are held by the indicated lenders are usually relatively high, in contrast to replies of farmers borrowing from other sources. It seems unlikely, however, that there would be any appreciable difference in this bias among the several counties.

Estimates of bank holdings of farm mortgage debt are based on the same types of data as those described above, but the method of adjustment was different. Farm real estate loans reported by banks located in the respective counties provided the starting point for these estimates; the second basis was the replies of farm owners to mailed questionnaires. Where the two bases disagreed markedly, data for the counties were further analyzed to produce a compromise estimate. Although the possible error in individual county estimates was reduced by the use of these independent bases, a substantial element of judgment necessarily entered into the estimates for a few of the counties.

The estimates for insurance companies, mortgage investment companies, and the residual group of miscellaneous and individual lenders represent a segment of farm mortgage debt not accounted for by land banks, the Federal Farm Mortgage Cor-

175

poration, or commercial banks on the basis of survey data obtained from farm owners. Since no independent check on the survey data could be made for these two major groups, the possibility of error in evaluating their loan percentages for individual counties is greater than that for the other two lender groups. However, the importance of insurance and mortgage investment company loans varies widely among counties, so that substantial differences in the estimated percentages of total mortgage debt held by the residual group may well represent nearly equal real differences.

NON-REAL-ESTATE LOANS OF THE
PRINCIPAL INSTITUTIONAL LENDERS

Data for PCA loans, FSA loans, and Emergency Crop and Feed loans are directly available for individual counties, but in a number of the drought-stricken counties the latter two classes of loans represented in 1940 an accumulation of past-due relief loans as well as current production loans. It is unlikely that the stratification of the sample for asset change in the 1930's fully offsets the distorting influence of these accumulated loans, but no basis was found on which to declare specific portions of the loans "dead debt" and to eliminate them from the total, especially since many of the debts incurred during the 1930's were repaid during the 1940's.

Data on non-real-estate loans of banks pertain to banks located in the county. Each county was separately considered from the viewpoint of the appropriateness of such data as a measure of current non-real-estate debt. Loan data of this type for counties in the range livestock area are particularly deficient; accordingly, after the counties were grouped, weight was given both to the ratio of loans to non-real-estate assets for the group and to the individual-county data in the estimates for individual counties. It is probable, however, that the result for this group of counties still underestimates the non-real-estate loans of banks in some of the counties, particularly where such loans are obtained from larger financial centers located outside the county.

APPENDIX B

SELECTED FINANCIAL DATA RELATING TO
AGRICULTURE BY STATES, 1930, 1940, AND 1950

ILLUSTRATIVE data by states which provide the basis for a comparison of 1940 with 1930 and 1950 with respect to certain financial characteristics of agriculture are shown in the accompanying table. For this purpose the states have been grouped into major types of farming regions.

The estimates of the distribution of interests in farm real estate among operators, landlords, and creditors require a brief explanation. The interest of operators represents the value of farm real estate in farms that are both owned and operated by the farm operator, less the estimated farm real estate debt of these farmers. For 1950 and 1940 the data for these estimates are available from *1950 Farm Mortgage Debt—Cooperative Report*, published in December 1952 by the Bureau of the Census and the Bureau of Agricultural Economics. For 1930 the estimates were made without the benefit of official state estimates of farm mortgage debt of part-owner farmers. However, the 1930 estimates are based on the same concepts as those employed for 1950 and 1940. Any lack of precision resulting from incompleteness of data in 1930 does not impair the usefulness of the data for general comparative purposes.

The estimates of the operator interest in farm real estate for all three base years tend to understate the extent of this interest. Any interest of farm operators in farms other than those operated by them, whether as landlord or as creditor, is excluded. Furthermore, the interest of operators in all farm assets on the farms they own (as well as operate) is a larger percentage of these assets than is their interest in the real estate alone. For example, tenant operators usually have a substantial interest in non-real-estate farm assets of the farms they operate. From our data for sample counties, it appears that operator interests in all farm assets exceeded 48 per cent in 1940 as compared with operator interests in farm real estate alone of less than 43 per cent.

If we subtract the estimated operator interest in farm real estate from total value of farm real estate, the residual becomes the combined interests of landlords and creditors. Again, if farm mortgage debt is subtracted from this residual, the remainder represents the landlord interest. The interests of operators who are also either landlords or creditors are classified with the landlord or creditor interest, as the case may be. It should be noted also that the landlord interest, as a residual, includes interests of different levels of government in farm land.

The additional state data shown in Table B-1 either are taken directly from published reports or are readily computed from such reports. The sources of these data are shown in the footnotes to these parts of the table.

TABLE B-1

Selected Financial Data Relating to Agriculture, by States, 1930, 1940, and 1950

Type of Farming Region and State	Value of Farm Real Estate[a] (land and buildings) (millions of dollars)			Interest of Farm Operators in Farm Real Estate[b] (per cent)			Interest of Landlords in Farm Real Estate[b] (per cent)			Interest of Creditors in Farm Real Estate[b] (per cent)			Percentage of Farms under Mortgage[e]			Ratio of Mortgage Debt to the Value of Mortgaged Farms[c] (per cent)			Percentage of Total Farm Mortgage Debt Held by Insurance Companies[d]		
	1950	1940	1930	1950	1940	1930	1950	1940	1930	1950	1940	1930	1950	1940	1930	1950	1940	1930	1950	1940	1930
Northeast																					
Maine	227	124	194	83.3	71.8	77.7	7.9	8.2	7.9	8.8	20.0	14.4	29.2	35.6	34.3	28.5	44.0	34.0	0.1	0.004	0.01
New Hampshire	125	62	77	76.0	70.9	70.4	11.2	11.1	14.0	12.8	18.0	15.6	40.1	42.6	38.6	31.4	40.0	36.1	0.03	0.00	0.0
Vermont	196	111	146	73.5	62.3	61.2	10.2	12.7	14.8	16.3	25.0	24.0	46.1	53.4	53.0	35.3	42.9	42.8	1.1	0.01	0.01
Massachusetts	315	212	261	74.9	61.8	62.7	12.7	16.6	18.5	12.4	21.6	18.8	46.9	53.6	54.2	28.2	41.6	35.9	1.6	0.02	0.04
Rhode Island	44	26	35	70.5	61.0	61.2	20.4	23.4	24.5	9.1	15.6	14.3	39.3	41.0	37.9	26.8	38.4	32.5	0.3	0.00	0.0
Connecticut	315	205	227	71.1	60.7	64.3	19.1	21.4	16.8	9.8	17.9	18.9	42.5	52.1	52.5	24.6	35.9	30.3	2.4	0.01	0.01
New York	1,467	947	1,316	72.3	61.5	59.8	16.2	18.7	22.4	11.5	20.3	17.8	39.5	46.1	45.4	30.7	41.6	38.7	4.5	0.1	0.1
New Jersey	505	228	299	71.1	56.6	56.8	17.8	22.0	25.1	11.1	21.4	18.1	39.5	49.7	50.8	27.1	41.4	36.8	13.4	0.3	0.4
Pennsylvania	1,513	864	1,203	69.9	61.2	61.9	20.3	23.6	24.5	9.8	15.2	14.0	29.1	33.3	34.3	32.8	42.5	36.3	3.4	0.6	0.4
Delaware	97	55	67	61.9	52.5	47.9	27.8	33.0	37.2	10.3	14.5	14.9	27.3	36.4	38.4	35.0	41.5	40.7	1.9	0.3	0.04
Maryland	512	280	363	62.3	52.8	51.0	27.2	30.5	35.2	10.5	16.7	13.8	32.9	37.4	37.9	31.6	42.2	38.8	6.5	4.9	1.4
Corn Belt																					
Ohio	2,859	1,444	1,693	56.2	50.2	49.8	35.8	33.2	34.1	8.0	16.6	16.1	29.5	37.0	35.6	30.3	41.7	42.9	11.8	13.6	21.7
Indiana	2,691	1,251	1,416	48.9	43.5	41.1	43.7	37.6	39.8	7.4	18.9	19.1	34.3	46.9	45.5	26.3	38.1	40.2	31.4	25.8	36.7
Illinois	5,395	2,537	3,336	33.7	29.9	29.3	61.4	53.6	52.3	4.9	16.5	18.4	23.5	34.9	40.7	26.4	42.6	43.8	34.1	26.9	29.6
Iowa	5,507	2,691	4,225	39.8	28.5	29.2	52.3	45.3	42.5	7.9	26.2	28.3	33.4	48.2	52.4	28.0	52.5	48.6	40.0	31.9	41.9
Missouri	2,236	1,107	1,796	58.7	41.4	43.4	33.8	37.9	31.9	7.5	20.7	24.7	31.5	42.4	44.9	26.8	48.1	45.3	39.6	27.4	32.9
Lake States																					
Michigan	1,701	913	1,161	69.0	58.4	55.1	21.8	22.5	25.9	9.2	19.1	19.0	31.4	45.5	49.0	31.2	41.1	41.6	4.0	2.0	3.7
Wisconsin	2,057	1,189	1,732	62.3	46.2	50.4	23.9	23.8	20.4	13.8	30.0	29.2	39.7	52.4	59.0	35.9	54.8	50.1	4.3	2.7	4.6
Minnesota	2,777	1,443	2,125	55.4	38.7	41.2	34.6	35.2	36.4	10.0	26.1	22.4	36.3	48.4	50.7	31.0	51.2	44.8	22.7	16.4	29.2
Great Plains																					
North Dakota	1,189	490	951	56.3	27.5	33.9	37.9	43.7	40.9	5.8	28.8	25.2	29.4	45.5	63.0	23.9	54.3	38.2	14.0	4.7	14.2
South Dakota	1,402	505	1,285	47.8	22.3	28.3	45.9	52.4	48.9	6.3	25.3	22.8	29.6	41.0	55.4	26.8	57.0	39.5	36.9	16.5	39.2
Nebraska	2,735	1,138	2,495	40.9	25.8	33.0	53.3	47.0	46.6	5.8	27.2	20.4	27.5	44.8	52.5	25.3	56.3	39.0	34.6	15.4	28.7
Kansas	3,199	1,421	2,281	42.1	31.5	34.6	53.4	48.5	47.3	4.5	20.0	18.1	26.1	44.6	41.3	25.9	44.0	35.6	30.8	19.6	36.5
Appalachian																					
West Virginia	487	270	342	81.1	71.5	71.9	13.8	20.4	20.5	5.1	8.1	7.6	15.6	19.3	18.4	27.6	33.7	31.0	1.5	2.7	1.8
Kentucky	1,572	776	871	64.1	58.2	59.0	29.3	27.7	27.7	6.6	14.1	13.3	19.1	26.6	24.0	27.2	36.9	36.2	19.3	13.5	22.7
Tennessee	1,432	664	743	63.9	55.3	52.2	30.0	30.8	32.3	6.1	13.9	15.5	20.1	30.1	24.4	27.4	36.5	36.0	13.5	16.0	33.0
Virginia	1,277	675	856	74.2	64.6	63.8	19.9	24.7	25.6	5.9	10.7	10.6	15.8	24.8	22.9	27.0	33.7	31.6	11.2	5.1	7.8
North Carolina	1,906	737	844	56.2	49.5	48.0	39.1	38.3	38.7	4.7	12.2	13.3	17.3	29.1	27.9	25.2	35.9	35.0	9.5	10.2	10.9

(concluded on next page)

TABLE B-1 (concluded)

Type of Farming Region and State	Value of Farm Real Estate[a] (land and buildings) (millions of dollars)			Interest of Farm Operators in Farm Real Estate[b] (per cent)			Interest of Landlords in Farm Real Estate[b] (per cent)			Interest of Creditors in Farm Real Estate[b] (per cent)			Percentage of Farms under Mortgage[c]			Ratio of Mortgage Debt to the Value of Mortgaged Farms[c] (per cent)			Percentage of Total Farm Mortgage Debt Held by Insurance Companies[d]		
	1950	1940	1930	1950	1940	1930	1950	1940	1930	1950	1940	1930	1950	1940	1930	1950	1940	1930	1950	1940	1930
Southeast																					
South Carolina	820	338	379	59.3	46.4	39.1	35.7	40.0	44.0	5.0	13.6	16.9	19.8	29.7	32.2	24.5	34.9	39.8	2.9	6.4	10.1
Georgia	1,115	480	577	59.2	39.7	35.1	33.3	43.2	45.3	7.5	17.1	19.6	26.3	34.3	31.2	28.5	39.4	39.7	12.7	16.8	25.5
Florida	946	324	423	65.0	56.4	35.1	28.0	31.9	32.4	7.0	11.7	12.5	24.0	32.8	26.0	22.3	28.5	26.6	16.8	2.1	4.4
Alabama	1,017	409	502	57.1	40.5	37.9	35.0	39.5	42.6	7.9	20.0	19.5	23.7	41.9	34.9	28.9	40.1	37.3	3.4	4.3	9.1
Delta																					
Mississippi	1,148	475	568	56.6	37.6	32.2	34.6	41.3	49.7	8.8	21.1	18.1	25.4	46.4	34.9	28.9	40.8	34.5	24.4	20.9	21.1
Louisiana	921	354	418	53.9	40.0	36.4	40.5	44.4	48.3	5.6	15.6	15.3	18.5	34.6	34.1	24.5	38.2	38.2	18.6	12.9	14.1
Arkansas	1,136	457	548	52.1	40.8	35.6	40.4	43.3	46.3	7.5	15.9	18.1	22.0	33.7	38.6	26.2	37.3	38.0	35.0	18.4	16.4
Oklahoma-Texas																					
Oklahoma	1,851	831	1,243	46.1	33.4	30.5	47.6	48.1	47.4	6.3	18.5	22.1	28.3	38.7	51.0	26.9	39.4	33.8	25.5	17.5	26.2
Texas	6,718	2,590	3,597	48.9	38.3	33.8	45.1	45.0	47.5	6.0	16.7	18.7	26.2	32.7	40.2	21.5	35.7	34.0	38.6	20.3	24.0
Mountain																					
Montana	999	350	528	59.0	42.1	37.8	34.8	39.0	37.6	6.2	18.9	24.6	30.9	43.4	53.2	25.3	38.7	40.1	11.2	5.6	8.6
Idaho	923	339	417	58.0	45.1	35.5	33.4	31.7	28.7	8.6	23.2	27.8	36.1	54.2	56.4	26.6	39.6	39.7	18.7	10.9	12.2
Wyoming	455	159	207	53.0	42.1	40.4	39.1	36.5	38.8	7.9	21.4	20.8	42.0	53.1	54.2	26.4	37.0	34.7	30.0	0.7	1.1
Colorado	1,212	388	629	50.8	36.7	34.7	40.5	44.0	43.4	8.7	19.3	21.9	38.5	44.4	51.1	27.6	42.2	39.3	20.2	4.7	5.0
New Mexico	713	188	208	52.9	49.3	39.8	40.4	36.0	41.4	6.7	14.7	18.8	29.4	26.2	25.1	25.4	30.4	39.3	45.8	9.0	10.6
Arizona	604	188	184	36.8	43.9	35.0	56.7	37.3	42.2	6.5	18.8	22.8	37.7	24.6	40.3	28.4	33.4	37.9	19.0	6.4	5.2
Utah	471	154	221	70.1	55.6	58.4	21.0	20.7	18.7	8.9	23.7	23.5	36.3	49.9	53.8	24.7	40.5	36.0	5.5	1.6	3.5
Nevada	136	48	64	59.6	51.2	45.2	30.8	27.3	29.8	9.6	21.5	25.0	32.2	37.8	44.2	31.0	38.9	41.2	25.9	5.3	3.1
Pacific																					
Washington	1,470	593	774	57.3	50.2	49.5	34.3	31.8	29.6	8.4	18.0	20.9	34.1	46.1	50.5	28.7	36.6	33.7	11.9	14.3	15.2
Oregon	1,216	477	631	65.0	53.2	50.3	25.5	27.8	28.1	9.5	19.0	21.6	37.0	48.1	51.5	28.3	35.1	34.6	12.7	9.2	10.4
California	5,650	2,166	3,419	54.8	47.0	46.1	37.0	34.2	35.9	8.2	18.8	18.0	38.1	49.2	52.5	25.0	35.3	32.0	13.6	3.7	3.7
United States	75,261	33,642	47,880	53.3	42.8	42.0	39.3	37.6	37.9	7.4	19.6	20.1	27.5	38.8	40.1	27.6	42.5	39.6	21.0	14.9	22.0

Sources:
a Bureau of the Census and Agricultural Research Administration.
b See text.
c *Census of Agriculture, 1950,* Vol. V, *Farm-Mortgage Debt,* Part 8.
d Harald C. Larsen, *Distribution by Lender Groups of Farm-Mortgage and Real Estate Holdings, January 1, 1930-45,* Dept. of Agriculture; *Farm-Mortgage Debt on January 1, 1953,* Dept. of Agriculture.

APPENDIX C

LIST OF COUNTIES INCLUDED IN
THE 108-COUNTY SAMPLE
BASIC TO THIS STUDY

ALABAMA
Etowah
Lee
Lowndes

ARIZONA
Yavapai

ARKANSAS
Benton
Bradley
Chicot
Crittenden
Independence

CALIFORNIA
Siskiyou

DELAWARE
Kent

FLORIDA
Suwannee

GEORGIA
Gordon
Greene
Jenkins
Wilcox

ILLINOIS
Douglas
Stark
Washington

INDIANA
Pike
Wayne

IOWA
Appanoose
Cherokee
Hamilton

KANSAS
Chautauqua
Decatur
Logan
Rush

KENTUCKY
Daviess
McCracken
Shelby

LOUISIANA
Jefferson Davis
Natchitoches
St. Landry

MARYLAND
Calvert
Frederick

MASSACHUSETTS
Hampden

MICHIGAN
Alpena
Calhoun
Mason
Sanilac
Shiawassee

MINNESOTA
Koochiching
Meeker
Polk
Winona

MISSISSIPPI
Coahoma
Lauderdale
Tishomingo
Warren

MISSOURI
Cass

MONTANA
Custer
Hill

NEBRASKA
Cheyenne
Dawes
Franklin
Pierce

NEVADA
Elko

NEW JERSEY
Cumberland

NEW MEXICO
Catron
San Miguel
Union

NEW YORK
Livingston

NORTH CAROLINA
Edgecombe

NORTH DAKOTA
Benson
Hettinger
Williams

OHIO
Morrow
Putnam
Trumbull

OKLAHOMA
Carter
Cleveland
Garfield
Washita

OREGON
Douglas
Union

PENNSYLVANIA
Blair
Chester
Tioga

SOUTH CAROLINA
Dillon
Kershaw

SOUTH DAKOTA
Day
Haakon
Hyde

TENNESSEE
Blount
Hardeman

TEXAS
Brewster
Burleson
DeWitt
Hansford
Kaufman
Lubbock
Nolan
Tom Green
Tyler

Upshur
Webb
Young

VERMONT
Orange

VIRGINIA
Prince Edward
Wythe

WASHINGTON
Adams

WEST VIRGINIA
Berkeley

WISCONSIN
Ashland
Dunn
Green
Winnebago
Wood

INDEX

Asset composition of farms:
  criteria and measurement of, 23 f., 170 f.
  cropland component, relation to financial organization, 64-67
  land component, relation to financial organization, 58-64
  for sample counties, 153 ff.
Asset deflation, farm, 1930-1940:
  and debt ratios, 36-38
  and distribution of interests in real estate among owners and creditors, 19-20, 139-140
  methods of adjusting for variations among counties, 35 ff.
  variation among sample counties, 37, 153 ff.
  variation among states, 18
Asset size of farms:
  financial organization of three different types of farms alike in average asset size, 77
  measurement of, 23-24, 170 f.
  and requirements for outside capital, 141 f.
  relation to economic and financial characteristics, 46-58, 63 f.

Barber, E. Lloyd, xi
Britt, Olive K., xii
Brody, Joan Janow, xii

County sample:
  adjustment for differences in financial experience in 1930's, 34-45
  basic estimates, 170 ff.
  comparisons with United States, 33
  geographical distribution, 32
  method of selection, 21, 31 f.
Credit use and changes in economic conditions, 139-140
Creditor interest in farm physical assets:
  derivation of estimates, 173-176
  real estate assets, 1930, 1940, 1950, by states, 179
  relation to economic characteristics, 89-96
  relation to total outside interests, 97-100

for selected counties, 89-92
Crop and livestock sales:
  and farm financial organization, 68-71
  financial patterns of crop and livestock counties compared, 69 f., 77

Dairy product sales:
  and farm financial organization, 71-80
  financial characteristics of large and small dairy farms, 75-76
  financial characteristics of small dairy farms and large crop farms, 79-80
  relation to sources of mortgage credit, 122
  relation to use of non-real-estate credit, 116
Diesslin, Howard G., 3
Durand, David, xi, 3

Economic characteristics of farms:
  comparison of sample counties with United States, 133
  indicators: for sample counties, 152-161; selection of, 23-26, 170-172
  relation to sources of mortgage credit, 121-127
  relation to use of non-real-estate credit, 113-119
  selected county illustrations, 26

Farm financial characteristics:
  indicators: for sample counties, 162-169; selection of, 27 f.
  interests of operators, landlords, and creditors in real estate, 1930, 1940, 1950, by states, 177-189
  relation of sources of mortgage credit, 123
  relation to use of non-real-estate credit, 116
  selected county illustrations, 29
Farm home consumption of farm products:
  basic data for sample counties, 158-161

183

RECENT AND FORTHCOMING
PUBLICATIONS OF THE
NATIONAL BUREAU OF ECONOMIC RESEARCH

NATIONAL BUREAU BOOKS *are available from bookstores or Princeton University Press, Princeton, New Jersey, except that contributors and subscribers to the National Bureau should order directly from the Bureau.* OCCASIONAL PAPERS, TECHNICAL PAPERS, *and* ANNUAL REPORTS *are available from the National Bureau of Economic Research, 261 Madison Avenue, New York 16, New York.*

BOOKS

Capital Formation in Residential Real Estate: Trends and Prospects (1956)	550 pp.	$10.00
Leo Grebler, David M. Blank, and Louis Winnick		
Trends in Employment in the Service Industries (1956)	188 pp.	3.75
George J. Stigler		
Consumption and Business Fluctuations: A Case Study of the Shoe, Leather, Hide Sequence (1956)	320 pp.	7.50
Ruth P. Mack		
Patterns of Farm Financial Structure: A Cross-Section View of Economic and Physical Determinants (1956)	206 pp.	4.50
Donald C. Horton		
The Pattern of Financial Asset Ownership: Wisconsin Individuals, 1949 (1956)	196 pp.	3.75
Thomas R. Atkinson		
Urban Mortgage Lending: Comparative Markets and Experience (1956)	212 pp.	4.00
J. E. Morton		
Personal Income during Business Cycles (1956)	208 pp.	4.00
Daniel Creamer		
Input-Output Analysis: An Appraisal (1955)	383 pp.	7.50
Studies in Income and Wealth, Volume Eighteen		
Short-Term Economic Forecasting (1955)	520 pp.	7.50
Studies in Income and Wealth, Volume Seventeen		
Minimum Price Fixing in the Bituminous Coal Industry (1955)	554 pp.	10.00
Waldo E. Fisher and Charles M. James		
Capital Formation and Economic Growth (1955)	691 pp.	12.00
Special Conference Series No. 6		
Business Concentration and Price Policy (1955)	524 pp.	9.00
Special Conference Series No. 5		
Long-Range Economic Projection (1954)	488 pp.	9.00
Studies in Income and Wealth, Volume Sixteen		
Mortgage Lending Experience in Agriculture (1954)	257 pp.	5.00
Lawrence A. Jones and David Durand		
The Frontiers of Economic Knowledge (1954)	376 pp.	5.00
Arthur F. Burns		
Regularization of Business Investment (1954)	539 pp.	8.00
Special Conference Series No. 4		
Shares of Upper Income Groups in Income and Savings (1953)	768 pp.	9.00
Simon Kuznets		
The Volume of Corporate Bond Financing since 1900 (1953)	464 pp.	7.50
W. Braddock Hickman		
Wesley Clair Mitchell: The Economic Scientist (1952)	398 pp.	4.00
Arthur F. Burns (ed.)		
A Study of Moneyflows in the United States (1952)	620 pp.	7.50
Morris A. Copeland		
The Trend of Government Activity in the United States since 1900 (1952)	288 pp.	4.00
Solomon Fabricant		
Federal Grants and the Business Cycle (1952)	136 pp.	2.00
James A. Maxwell		
Studies in Income and Wealth, Volume Fifteen (1952)	240 pp.	3.50
Eight papers on size distribution of income		

Conference on Research in Business Finance (1952)	360 pp.	$5.00
Special Conference Series No. 3		
Deterioration in the Quality of Foreign Bonds Issued in the		
United States, 1920-1930 (1951)	112 pp.	2.00
Ilse Mintz		

OCCASIONAL PAPERS

53. *Productivity Trends: Capital and Labor* (1956) $ .50
   John W. Kendrick
52. *Resource and Output Trends in the United States since 1870* .50
   Moses Abramovitz
51. *Interest as a Source of Personal Income and Tax Revenue* (1956) 1.25
   Lawrence H. Seltzer
50. *Agricultural Equipment Financing* (1955) 1.25
   Howard G. Diesslin
49. *The Korean War and United States Economic Activity,*
   1950-1952 (1955) .75
   Bert G. Hickman
48. *A Century and a Half of Federal Expenditures* (1955) 1.25
   M. Slade Kendrick
46. *Immigration and the Foreign Born* (1954) 1.50
   Simon Kuznets and Ernest Rubin
45. *Capital and Output Trends in Mining Industries, 1870-1948*
   (1954) 1.00
   Israel Borenstein
44. *The Growth of Physical Capital in Agriculture, 1870-1950* (1954) 1.25
   Alvin S. Tostlebe
43. *Trends and Cycles in Capital Formation by United States Railroads,*
   1870-1950 (1954) 1.50
   Melville J. Ulmer
42. *The Share of Financial Intermediaries in National Wealth and*
   National Assets, 1900-1949 (1954) 1.50
   Raymond W. Goldsmith
41. *Capital and Output Trends in Manufacturing Industries,*
   1880-1948 (1954) 1.50
   Daniel Creamer
30. *Costs and Returns on Farm Mortgage Lending by Life Insurance*
   Companies, 1945-1947 (1949) 1.00
   R. J. Saulnier

TECHNICAL PAPERS

11. *Fiscal-Year Reporting for Corporate Income Tax* (1956) $1.25
   W. L. Crum
10. *Factors Influencing Consumption: An Experimental*
   Analysis of Shoe Buying (1954) 2.00
   Ruth P. Mack
9. *The Volume of Residential Construction, 1889-1950* (1954) 1.50
   David M. Blank

ANNUAL REPORTS (GRATIS)

By Solomon Fabricant
36th. *Basic Research and the Analysis of Current Business Conditions* (May 1956)
35th. *Government in Economic Life* (May 1955)

This book may be kept